Electric locomotive No 3 pauses for a short while during trial runs on the Simpasture Branch c1915. Taken at Preston Lane crossing (looking west). *(Courtesy: NRM, York)*

SHILDON~NEWPORT IN RETROSPECT

The fore-runner of Main Line Electrification

Electric Locomotive No 8 at Newport 12th October 1921 with dynamometer car attached to train of mineral empties for Shildon (note Newport Shed). *(Courtesy: K.L. Taylor)*

K.C. APPLEBY

THE RAILWAY CORRESPONDENCE AND TRAVEL SOCIETY

1990

ISBN 0 901115 67 3

Published by the Railway Correspondence and Travel Society
21 Winthorpe Road, Lincoln LN6 3PG

COVER DESIGN BY JOHN HOLROYD

Photoset in 9/10 Plantin

Printed by AB Printers Ltd, Leicester

Contents

SHILDON-NEWPORT IN RETROSPECT

PREFACE

My initial memories of the Shildon-Newport line go back to 1935. During the summer of that year I witnessed the dismantling of overhead electrification equipment along our local mineral railway which passed close to Ropner Park near my home at Stockton-on-Tees. Much to my regret I cannot recall ever seeing the electric trains in action, and upon reflection perhaps I was rather too young at the time to properly appreciate the significance of what was happening. It was I suppose, difficult to understand why anything electric — which in the 1930s was regarded as 'modern' — was being removed, and why had steam power replaced the erstwhile electrically hauled mineral trains? These questions were to remain unanswered for many years.

Now over half a century later, my dormant interest has been revived, and after much research it has become possible to piece together a fairly comprehensive story about the now largely defunct Shildon-Newport route. The rise and fall of the short lived electrification scheme between 1915 and 1935 has a particular fascination, being the first example in this country of electric traction used for mineral traffic haulage. Then the route itself was steeped in history with much of it having its origins in two of the North East's earliest railways — the famous Stockton and Darlington of 1825 and the less well known Clarence of 1833. A portion of the route, however, dated from a much later North Eastern inspired expansion during the 1870s.

The fortunes of the Shildon-Newport route tended to follow those of the South West Durham coalfield and the iron and steel industry on Tees-side. The late 19th century was a boom period as the volume of rail-borne traffic grew commensurate with increased industrial activity in the area which reached its peak by 1913. The Shildon-Newport line was electrified in 1915 — this being a pioneer scheme which soon became the proving ground for Sir Vincent Raven's ultimate objective of main line electrification between York and Newcastle. While the electrification was in itself a technical success, the harsh economic realities of life encountered during the trade depression of the 1920s and 30s took their toll upon the railway's freight business — so much so that by 1935 electric traction was abandoned as it had long ceased to be a commercially viable proposition.

An upsurge in activity took place during World War II; indeed part of the original 1833 Clarence Railway (known as the Simpasture Branch) even saw passenger trains again after almost 100 years following construction of a large ordnance factory at Aycliffe. But the post-war era saw a sharp decline in output from the South West Durham coalfield followed by numerous pit closures. Equally during the 1950s and 60s radical changes took place in the shape and form of the Tees-side iron and steel industry which completely transformed the pattern of freight movement by rail in this particular corner of the North East.

The resultant decline during the mid-1960s was followed by an almost inevitable rationalisation of railway facilities, thus the axe fell upon much of the Shildon-Newport line in this period. A lot of this once busy freight and mineral artery has already passed into oblivion, hence all the more reason why this story needs to be written before traces vanish and memories fade.

Closely associated with the Shildon-Newport story is the Castle Eden Branch, the northern extremity of which reached as far as Wellfield, yet it enjoyed the status of a secondary main line until the coast route between West Hartlepool and Seaham was completed in 1905. This line arose from North Eastern Railway expansion of the late 1870s but declined into a little known railway backwater which closed in 1966. In parts it has almost disappeared though a delightful stretch between Thorpe Thewles and Wynyard is now known as the 'Castle Eden Walkway'.

This work is dedicated to numerous railwaymen friends and colleagues, both past and present, particularly those around Tees-side who over the years sustained my historical interest. Acknowledgement is also due for research facilities afforded by the ever helpful staff of the National Railway Museum York, County Records Office Durham, and Public Record Office Kew. Mr Chris Jackson, Production Editor of Railway Gazette International, kindly gave permission to use certain archive material and photographs as did Mr D.J. Butler, Durham County

Archivist, Mr A.J. Roberts, Chief Executive Officer of Sedgefield District Council, and Mr Robert Anderson of British Rail's photographic unit in York. Sincere thanks for their assistance also go to several fellow members of the Signalling Record Society, Mr Ken Taylor of the North Eastern Railway Association and Mr David Tyreman of the RCTS.

Finally, I was most grateful to the doyen of North Eastern historians — the late Mr Ken Hoole — for initial help and encouragement, and I was similarly indebted to that other faithful recorder of the ever changing North Eastern scene — the late Mr J.W. Armstrong. Acknowledgements are also due to Messrs Reg Sowler, Ray Goad, John Boyes and to the many other photographers whose work is individually credited in the captions.

YORK   K.C. APPLEBY
September 1990

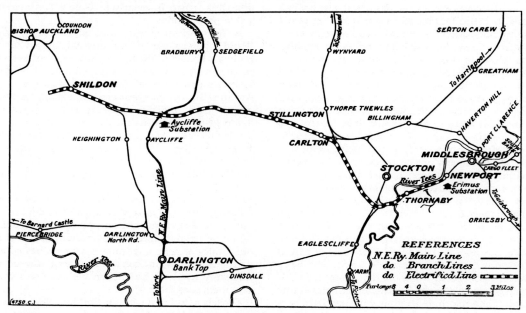

Fig. 1   Shildon-Newport location map.   (Courtesy: British Rail)

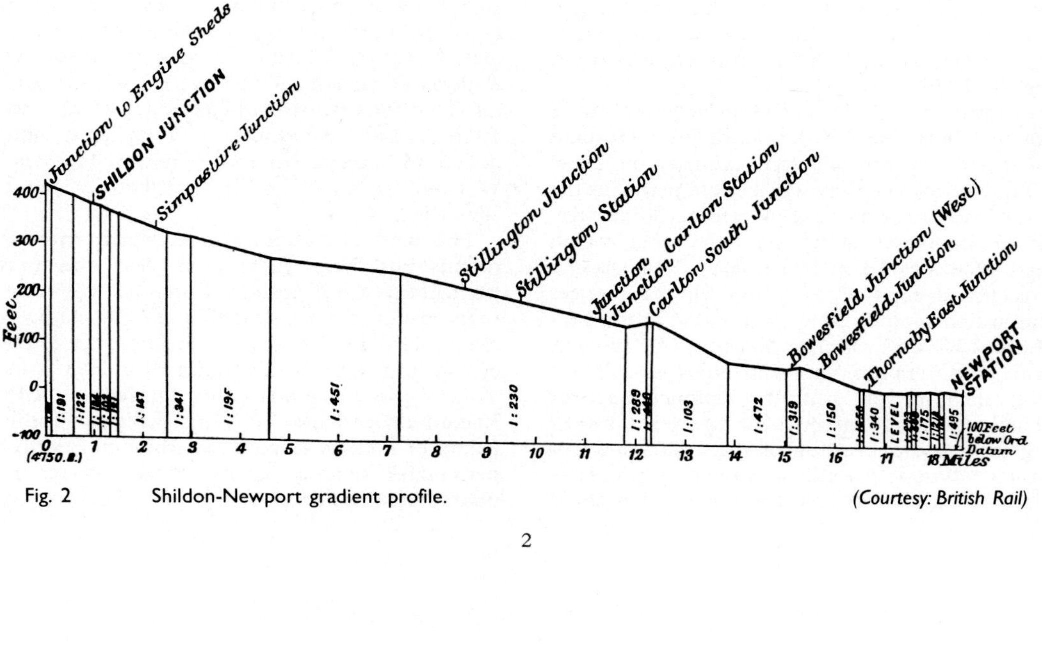

Fig. 2   Shildon-Newport gradient profile.   (Courtesy: British Rail)

1. THE BEGINNINGS — EARLY HISTORY TO 1865

Both extremities of the Shildon-Newport route were in Stockton and Darlington Railway territory. The Shildon end was the original S&D line which opened on 27th September 1825 when the inaugural train hauled by *Locomotion No 1* commenced its epic journey from Shildon (Mason's Arms Crossing) to Stockton. At the Stockton end where the 1825 S&D bound for the riverside wharves crossed Bowesfield Lane, (at a location soon to become known as Bowesfield Junction), the Middlesbrough Extension left the original route and shortly afterwards crossed over the River Tees by a short lived suspension bridge. This the first of many S&D inspired extensions opened on 27th December 1830, and its objective was to develop a new site on the Yorkshire bank of the Tees, downstream from Stockton, to be known as 'Port Darlington' — or Middlesbrough as it soon became.

Diverging from the S&D at Simpasture Junction, in the vicinity of the present Newton Aycliffe Halt, was the Clarence Railway of 1833 (known later as the Simpasture Branch) and for the next 6 miles or so it headed eastwards bound for a location known as Stillington Moor House where its so-called City of Durham Branch of 1834 came in at Stillington Junction (Stillington North since 1928). Then for some 4 miles towards Carlton (Redmarshall from 1923) the Clarence headed for Stockton (North Shore) and Samphire Batts (soon to become Port Clarence).

At Carlton West Junction, the 1877 Castle Eden Branch of the NER turned off southwards from the Clarence main line and passing to the west of Stockton it joined the erstwhile S&D at Bowesfield Junction. The Castle Eden Branch — the 'Cuckoo Railway' to many local residents but the 'Eden' to most railwaymen! — also extended in 1878 for some 10 miles northwards from the junctions at Carlton to Castle Eden North Junction (Wellfield from 1882), where it joined a much earlier railway system from Hartlepool which had penetrated into the Central Durham coalfield.

Much has been written about the Stockton and Darlington Railway and its well chronicled opening day — particularly so around the time of the 1925 Railway Centenary celebrations and, more recently, the commemoration of Rail 150 in 1975. Its early history has been thoroughly researched and fully

documented. The Clarence has not, however, received quite the same degree of published attention from railway historians, and in the context of the Shildon-Newport story one must briefly consider the general background as to why the S&D and Clarence Railways came into being in the first place and also look at the business and civic rivalries which existed between the towns of Stockton and Darlington. Indeed, it is necessary to recount in some detail the ups and downs of Clarence Railway affairs during its relatively short period of separate existence.

The saga begins in the early 19th century with the River Tees itself. The Tees followed a lengthy and meandering course of about 15 miles between Stockton and the sea which made it a difficult river to navigate, especially so around the two great loops just downstream from Stockton. Shipping was a painfully slow and hazardous operation hence enterprising businessmen of the day were seeking to improve contemporary methods of transport, particularly concerning the movement and export of coal from the developing South West Durham coalfield around Shildon and Bishop Auckland. At that time Stockton was an ancient port of some importance and proposals were made for improved navigation designed to artificially straighten out the winding course of the Tees and deepen the waterway by dredging. Two cuts were made below Stockton which effectively shortened the distance to the sea by some 3 miles; the first of 154 yards known as the 'Mandale Cut' was opened on 18th September 1810 and the second, the 'Portrack Cut', 725 yards long followed on 10th February 1831. In an attempt to improve inland communications the opposing ideas of a canal versus railway were well and truly ventilated, and as this story has been more than adequately told before suffice it to say that the railway protagonists won the day — hence the S&D which came into being in 1825. The S&D, led by Edward Pease a notable Darlington businessman and prominent Quaker, was very much Darlington orientated (sometimes called the 'Quaker Railway'!) and even before the line was opened in 1825, the Pease influence on the S&D Board resulted in the planning of a venture down river from Stockton where coal shipment facilities potentially superior to those at Stockton might be established.

3

Fig. 3   Masons Arms level crossing looking east c1895 (this is the location at Shildon from where the inaugural S&D train commenced its epic journey in 1825). *(Courtesy: K.L. Taylor collection)*

Fig. 4   Masons Arms level crossing looking west c1925 (note overhead electrification safety guard). *(Courtesy: K.L. Taylor collection)*

In those early days much rivalry, even distrust, existed between the 'Darlington' and 'Stockton' factions, so much so that even as far back as 1819 another railway (known as the 'Northern' route) had been proposed independently of the projected S&D to link the coalfield and the Tees. The origins of the Clarence Railway can thus be traced back to 1819 and to the proposed Tees and Weardale Railway, notices for which appeared on 13th September 1823. This line, which was promoted by much the same people as those associated with the so-called 'Northern' route of 1819, was to run from Willington (between Bishop Auckland and Durham) to the north bank of the Tees at Billingham Reach (near Haverton Hill) via Mainsforth near Ferryhill, but its parliamentary bill was defeated on 19th February 1824 following strong opposition from the S&D whose railway by then was in an advanced state of construction.

This parliamentary defeat, probably the first example of inter-railway rivalry even before railways in the accepted sense existed, did not deter the Tees and Weardale promoters whose ranks were strengthened by Mr Christopher Tennant of Yarm a public spirited gentleman who championed Stockton's interests (and subsequently those of Hartlepool!). Tennant was disenchanted with the Darlington faction of the S&D and had become disillusioned with the way things seemed to be going. Stockton had not yet got its railway — nor indeed its second River Tees cut — yet its future prospects looked very much like being adversely affected by a Darlington inspired extension down river. Originally the S&D had thought of extending to somewhere on the north bank around Haverton Hill but after it became apparent that the proposed extension on the south bank to Middlesbrough was the preferred option, Tennant threw in his lot with the 'Northern' camp and brought forward a scheme which proved to be the genesis of the Clarence Railway.

A second and revised Tees & Weardale bill was presented in parliament during 1824/25. Its professed objective was to convey coal from the Coxhoe area and physical connection with the S&D was not originally contemplated. In the event opposition to it was so strong, not only from the S&D but from coal owners along the Wear and Tyne that the bill was thrown out on 14th May 1825, emphasising yet again the degree of antagonism and fear of competition which existed in those days even before the railway as an effective transport mode had actually proved itself.

Undeterred, Tennant and the 'Stockton' faction pressed forward with yet another proposed railway. This time, because the line was not actually going into Weardale the old title was considered inappropriate, and as Tennant in his younger days had served in the Navy the new name he chose was the 'Clarence Railway' — so called after the Duke of Clarence, then Lord High Admiral of the Fleet (later to become King William IV 1830-1837). The proposed Clarence Railway was intended to tap the Auckland coalfield by means of the Deanery Branch (situated slightly north east of Shildon) and run direct to Haverton Hill with branches to Durham and Stockton. A connection with the S&D was envisaged at 'Sim Pasture' (Simpasture) and the Clarence Railway bill was passed — despite strong opposition — on 23rd May 1828. Stockton supported the Clarence as strongly as Darlington opposed it. By this time the S&D had gone ahead with a bill for its Middlesbrough extension and a business consortium headed by Edward Pease (the 'Middlesbrough Owners') was in the process of purchasing a substantial amount of land on the south bank of the Tees for development of new port facilities and creation of a new town (Middlesbrough). In an attempt to improve its shipping potential, Stockton was proceeding with a second cut in the river (the Portrack cut of 1831), but already the days of Stockton as a major port for coal shipment were numbered!

The ink was hardly dry upon the original Clarence Railway Act of Authorisation passed in 1828, when doubts arose as to whether after all their engineer, Mr Edward Steel, had selected the best course. The directors then consulted Mr George Leather of Leeds, the engineer for the original Tees and Weardale projected line, who suggested several significant alterations. This meant an amended proposal had to be made through parliamentary channels, and the Royal Assent was finally received on 1st June 1829, with work actually commencing in 1830. In the event, delay ensued in digging out cuttings and making up embankments. Then it was found that independent access to the Auckland coalfield could not be achieved via the proposed Deanery Branch, construction of which involved driving a tunnel underneath Lord Eldon's estate in order to reach places north and west of Shildon. Lord Eldon's objections were so strong (and so well supported!) that the Clarence was forced to abandon the Deanery Branch thus it was left with the Simpasture connection as the only means of reaching its goal. So the Clarence became inextricably linked with its arch rival the S&D, and rather like the Hull & Barnsley some 50 years later it had to make do with a second best alternative and be content with terminating just short of its originally intended destination.

Predominantly a mineral line, the Clarence opened in August 1833 when its first delivery of landsale coal was made at Stockton. Detailed

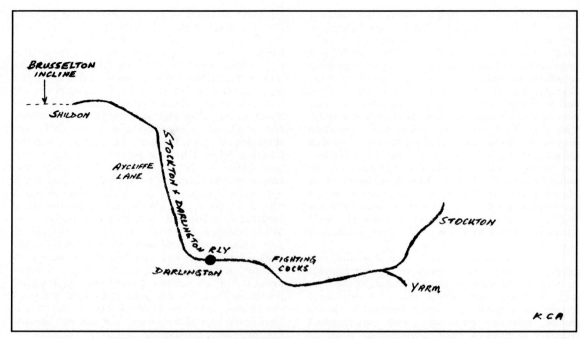

Drawing 1   SHILDON-NEWPORT ROUTE SKETCH IN 1825 — Only the S&D was then in existence.

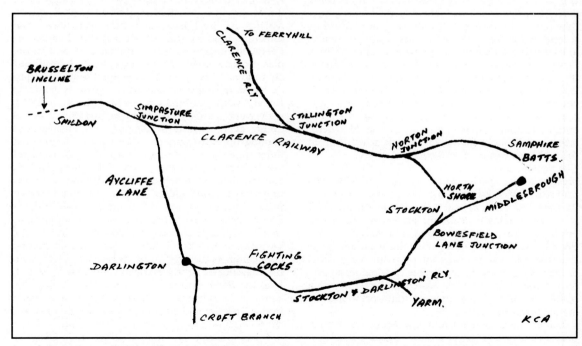

Drawing 2   SHILDON-NEWPORT ROUTE SKETCH IN 1834 — After the Clarence Railway had arrived on the scene.

research has so far failed to find a precise opening date, though it is recorded that the first delivery of coal for shipment reached Stockton on 29th October 1833. Thus the year 1833 marked the beginning of a new era in 19th century railway history. Here at Simpasture, just south east of Shildon, were the first examples of a junction between two rival companies and the start of inter-railway competition. In theory the Clarence held a superior position to the S&D having the benefit of a shorter route by some 6 miles to the Tees at Stockton, but this inbuilt advantage could not be exploited because of the ill-feeling and suspicion, even open distrust, which existed between the rival protagonists. A real struggle for revenue between the two companies began in 1833 which continued unabated for the rest of the Clarence Railway's separate existence.

By 16th January 1834, the City of Durham Branch of the Clarence Railway had been opened between Stillington Junction and Thrislington (near Ferryhill). At the eastern end the line from a junction with the Stockton Branch (now known as Norton West) to Haverton Hill was opened on 30th January 1834 and a few months later it was extended to Samphire Batts (Port Clarence), a better termination point where ships could lie afloat at any state of tide.

Originally built as a single track with passing places at intervals of about every mile, the line fell gently from Simpasture towards Stockton and Port Clarence. Horses were first employed throughout but following a lot of remedial work on cuttings and bank strengthening between 1833 and 1836 the line was doubled and locomotives introduced. Both locomotives and horses were used from 1836, but by 1841 the horses had disappeared, not surprisingly when one considers that the authorised mineral train loadings with locomotives were 32 wagons equal to 136 tons laden weight and 51 empties in the reverse direction. A feature peculiar to the Clarence (and different from the S&D) was that in its very early days trains ran on the right — just as they did originally on the Newcastle and Carlisle Railway!

Although first and foremost a mineral railway, the Clarence ventured into the passenger business between Stockton (North Shore) and Coxhoe (for Durham) from 11th July 1835, but its original 'main line' via Simpasture only saw passenger services for a very brief period between 30th November 1841 and 12th February 1842. This short lived passenger service was actually S&D inspired being operated by S&D locomotives and coaches running between Darlington (North Road) and Coxhoe (for Durham) involving reversals at both Simpasture and Stillington junctions, one of the very few examples of S&D and Clarence co-operation. This circuitous operation failed to pay its way and was probably the first known case of a passenger service withdrawal.

Relationships between the Clarence and S&D companies never really improved — apart from the foregoing brief venture into passenger operation. Right from the outset in 1833 there was a rates war which not unnaturally favoured the S&D who held control of the traffic coming on to the system at Shildon. In the struggle for revenue, the S&D prohibited horse leaders on and off the Clarence line at Simpasture from operating during the hours of darkness (even though the S&D did not so prohibit their own horsemen) and S&D loaded wagons were just counted past Thickley Weigh siding (located in what later became part of the Shildon marshalling yard complex) whereas wagons destined for the Clarence route had to be individually weighed which slowed things down considerably and resulted in congestion.

It was inevitable that such a state of affairs would soon lead the Clarence into deep financial trouble. In fact the Clarence was busily extending in other directions with branches to Sherburn (1835) — which actually got no further than Coxhoe — Chilton (1836) and Byers Green (1837). Its City of Durham Branch (1834) reached Thrislington (just north of Ferryhill) but never got to its intended destination. Over extended, under capitalised and starved of revenue, despite its geographical advantage of distance over the S&D, and constantly engaged in litigation with its neighbours the Clarence sunk further and further into the red. Added to this, many of its engineering works needed substantial rectification at considerable expense, so much so that on 31st July 1834 the Clarence, unable to repay interest on its borrowings, asked a body then known as the Exchequer Loan Commission to take control of its financial affairs. (In a last ditch attempt to raise more capital the Clarence had even resorted to the creation of additional shares at a discount of 65% — thus saddling themselves with £100 of liability for every £35 received!) The centre of administration and financial control thus moved to London — perhaps the cause of even further managerial problems?

Matters came to a head with the celebrated Simpasture 'incident' of 1837. At that time the S&D were phasing out horses in favour of locomotives but would not allow the Clarence to haul traffic with their own locomotives between Simpasture and the foot of Brusselton and Black Boy inclines at Shildon. (There were no such things as 'Running Powers' agreements in those early days.) On 12th September 1837 the Clarence attempted to run a train through to Shildon with their locomotive *Sir Robert Peel* but this was thwarted by S&D employees who effectively removed a rail. The S&D thereafter stationed 'two men' at the junction to prevent any further such attempts by the Clarence.

Meanwhile Christopher Tennant was active in promoting a railway to Hartlepool and a line first known as the Clarence and Hartlepool Union Railway was proposed to branch off the Clarence at Billingham and run to what later became known as West Hartlepool. Opened on 12th November 1840 (for goods) and 9th February 1841 (for passengers) as the Stockton and Hartlepool Railway, the struggling Clarence was leased to the new company for 21 years as from September 1844. Unfortunately Tennant did not live to see the outcome of his endeavours — he died in 1839 — but his work was carried on by Sir Ralph Ward Jackson who was responsible for the subsequent development of a new town called West Hartlepool just as Edward Pease had been instrumental in the creation of Middlesbrough.

Still at odds with all and sundry, relations between the Clarence and their new lessees (the Stockton and Hartlepool) were soon strained by the diversion of coal shipments from Port Clarence to Hartlepool, but subsequently Jackson secured on behalf of the Stockton and Hartlepool Railway a permanent lease of the Clarence effective from 1st January 1851. Six months later on 1st July 1851, the unification of the Stockton and Hartlepool with the Hartlepool West Harbour and Dock Company took place, confirmed by Royal Assent on 30th June 1852, thus signalling the end of the Clarence Railway as an independent concern. From 17th May 1853 the Clarence became part of the newly formed West Hartlepool Harbour and Railway Company which in turn amalgamated with the North Eastern Railway on 1st July 1865.

The S&D on the other hand was a thriving concern which expanded in all directions. By 1862 it had extended to such widely diverse places as Saltburn and Guisborough in the east, and Penrith and Tebay in the west. It also reached into Weardale as far as Stanhope and its influence stretched northwards via Crook and Tow Law to Consett. The S&D had also established extensive workshops at Shildon for the building and repair of locomotives and rolling stock and was actively engaged in building a new locomotive works at Darlington (North Road). By mid-19th century standards the S&D was certainly big business.

Amalgamation of the S&D with the North Eastern became effective from 1st July 1863, thus from 1865 the lines of two erstwhile fiercely competitive rivals for the growing coal traffic between South West Durham and Tees-side at last came under one unified management. Simpasture Junction, the first example of inter-railway competition ceased to be a 'frontier point' and the 30 years rates war came to an end.

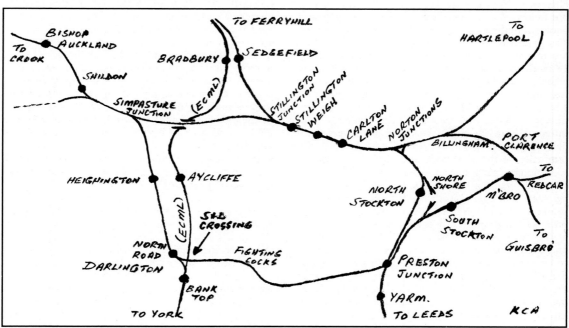

Drawing 3   SHILDON-NEWPORT ROUTE SKETCH IN 1854 — When the North Eastern Railway was formed.

2. NORTH EASTERN RAILWAY: EXPANSION TO 1913

The volume of railborne mineral traffic which originated in South West Durham grew by leaps and bounds throughout the latter part of the 19th century. Not only was there an ever increasing tonnage of coal being produced for industrial use, but as the iron and steel industry firmly established itself on Tees-side so a further demand grew for the conveyance of limestone and other minerals — particularly from Weardale. It soon became evident that the provision of additional facilities was necessary for the purpose of gathering together the output from an expanding network of rail connected collieries, coke ovens and quarries situated to the north and west of Shildon, and to facilitate the return of empty wagons for distribution.

In the mid-1860s a start was made on the construction of a large marshalling yard at Shildon, the chosen site south east of Shildon being in the vicinity of the Thickley Weigh sidings where traffic had been exchanged between the S&D and Clarence Railways right from the beginning. A large area of land was acquired for the construction of reception and sorting sidings and it was here the first known example of gravitation shunting could be found, the

yard being situated on a generally falling gradient which averaged 1 in 144. The passenger lines were slued round the perimeter of the new yard, known as the 'laden yard', which opened during 1869 and dealt with upwards of 2000 wagons per day. By the mid-1870s following the acquisition of more land, the actual junction between the S&D and Clarence lines was moved 49 chains nearer Shildon from the original meeting place between the two routes, thus the ex-Clarence tracks ran parallel with those of the S&D to a resited Simpasture Junction. Round about the same time a new yard for empty wagons was opened, entered from Middridge (mid-way between the resited Simpasture Junction and Shildon), thus the passenger lines then ran through the middle of a large yard complex.

Another feature of note is that by 1863 the Hartburn Curve had been constructed at Stockton. This linked the former Leeds Northern line of 1852 (which ran from Melmerby via Northallerton to Stockton North Shore Junction where it joined the Clarence) to the S&D system at Bowesfield. Traffic could then run from the Shildon area to Tees-side via the ex-Clarence Railway Simpasture Branch, as

Fig. 5   Shildon Marshalling Yards around the turn of the century — looking towards Middridge ('Laden' yard to left of picture and 'Empties' yard to right.)

(Courtesy: K.L. Taylor collection)

9

well as via the traditional S&D route, which from 1844 had suffered from the disadvantage of being crossed on the level just north of Darlington by the then new main line between York and Newcastle. In fact, following the two rival companies being amalgamated with the North Eastern in 1863/1865, the Simpasture Branch then became the favoured route.

By the 1870s it had become painfully obvious that the over-burdened railway system and its inadequate terminal facilities within the growing industrial Tees-side complex was being stretched to the limit. Additionally there was by then a heavy volume of traffic passing from the Ferryhill direction (over the erstwhile Clarence Railway City of Durham Branch) which converged with the Simpasture Branch at Stillington Junction. Yet another factor stemmed from the further development of the Durham coalfield in the centre of the county, and as the only available rail outlets towards the Tees were either via Ferryhill or Hartlepool, the North Eastern proposed in 1870 the building of a completely new railway from Castle Eden North Junction (renamed Wellfield from 1882) to Carlton (renamed Redmarshall from 1923) and Stockton (Bowesfield Junction). This was known as the Castle Eden Branch (authorised by NER Act of 1872); it joined the ex-S&D network at Bowesfield, and also connected with the ex-Clarence route by means of north to east and west to south curves at Carlton. The first section to open was that from Carlton West to Bowesfield on 1st May 1877, and it afforded immediate relief because it effectively by-passed the congested Stockton area. This was closely followed by the Castle Eden North Junction (Wellfield) to Carlton South line from 1st August 1878 and at the same time the curves from Carlton North to East and Wingate South to Wingate were opened — the latter to gain access to and from the Ferryhill-Hartlepool route.

Concurrently with these developments — in still another attempt to improve line capacity — the North Eastern quadrupled certain sections of track around Tees-side during the 1873-1876 period, notably from Stockton Cut (West of Bowesfield) to Tees Bridge, also between South Stockton (later called Thornaby) and Newport. Land was acquired in the Newport area to permit construction of a large marshalling yard to complement that at Shildon, which involved the first of three diversions of the passenger lines as the original 1830 S&D (Middlesbrough extension) formation passed right through the site. Whereas Shildon yard was built on a falling gradient favourable for gravitation shunting, the site at Newport along the foreshore of the Tees and largely situated on reclaimed marshland was virtually level, thus artificial gradients had to be created using slag from a nearby ironworks — so

here was a very early example of a hump yard. Newport yard opened to traffic on 16th November 1875 and sufficient land had also been reserved for the building of a large engine shed to service the ever increasing traffic needs. The new shed was opened in 1881, but by 1888 it had become unsafe due to subsidence, so by 1890 a newer much enlarged shed had to be provided.

Despite the effects of a trade recession during the 1870s this particular corner of the North Eastern's empire became busier than ever and in yet another attempt to increase line capacity an ambitious quadrupling scheme was embarked upon over the four miles between Carlton West and Stillington Junction, powers being obtained by NER Act of 1876 and a contract for construction awarded to Messrs Walter Scott of Newcastle in 1882.

By that time the community now known as Stillington had just grown up around the Carlton Ironworks first established in 1866 (and not actually situated at Carlton!). A new station called Carlton Ironworks had been opened in the early 1870s as the original Clarence Railway station known as Stillington was actually located much nearer to Stillington Junction (at a site known as 'Stillington Weigh'). From 1st November 1879 the old station fell into disuse and Carlton Ironworks station was renamed Stillington. Construction of the new mineral lines involved the provision of new passenger stations at Stillington and Carlton (Redmarshall) — both being of the island platform type. The new mineral lines, which enabled parallel working of trains between the Simpasture Branch and Newport simultaneously with movements between Ferryhill and Norton West were opened around 1885, though considerable research has so far failed to produce anything better than Board of Trade inspection dates of 9th February and 6th May 1884. A further modification to this widening scheme occurred some ten years later when the junction and signal box at Carlton West was abolished, the physical connection between the Norton West and Bowesfield routes then being transferred to Carlton Station (Redmarshall) where the box was extended and resignalled for a completely new layout of two double junctions (inspected by the Board of Trade on 26th September 1895).

Then in 1900 a new spur to be known as the Hartburn West Curve was proposed to link up the former Leeds Northern line at Hartburn West Junction with the Castle Eden Branch at Bowesfield West, the object being to allow certain through services to and from the Sunderland direction to avoid Stockton. This very short lived curve was, according to letters from the North Eastern Railway to the Board of Trade dated 2nd August and 25th September 1900 "completed but not maintained for passenger traffic for the present" and it passed its Board of Trade inspection on 17th August 1901. Some sources suggest the curve was opened from 11th February 1901 — and this may well be correct — but apart from infrequent use by express freight trains between Sunderland and the South until 1903, the curve served no other purpose. The box called Hartburn West on the Leeds Northern line is known to have been closed by 1904. (It has also been suggested that the Stockton Chamber of Trade expressed grave concern at their town possibly being by-passed!)

To return to Bowesfield Junction; a new Tees viaduct parallel with the 1844 replacement of the original 1830 suspension bridge was planned to enable the piecemeal quadrupling to be completed throughout between Bowesfield and Newport, and a contract awarded to Walter Scott of Newcastle on 21st October 1880. (Incidentally the 1844 replacement bridge carrying the passenger lines over the Tees was itself replaced in 1907.)

Major alterations also took place around South Stockton (Thornaby) during the early 1880s. Two heavily used level crossings at Mandale Road and Thornaby Road were swept away in the construction of two new overbridges, and a large island platform station was opened on 1st October 1882. This was situated immediately adjacent to the former single platform station which could no longer cope with the frequent passenger service interspersed with an almost continuous procession of slow moving freights. Furthermore the old station had to be demolished because it stood in the way of the new mineral lines which were opened throughout in 1883. It is also of interest to note that the expanding

community known as South Stockton became a separate borough in its own right on 6th October 1892 taking the name 'Thornaby', and the new station was so renamed from 1st November 1892.

During the early years of the 20th century further major expansion took place at Newport as Tees-side's railway system grew busier than ever. Not only was there the heavy Shildon-Newport traffic flow but enormous quantities of raw materials and other merchandise entered the area from the north and south all of which had to pass Bowesfield Junction. Added to this, heavy tonnages of Cleveland ironstone, domestic to Tees-side, were moved by rail, mostly in block train loads direct to the various works, and large numbers of empty iron and steel carrying wagons required to be collected and segregated for supply to the various works in the locality. On the outwards side vast quantities of finished iron and steel products were despatched by rail (mainly loaded in works private sidings) together with quite a lot of inter-works movements. All this freight activity added up to a pressing need for even better marshalling facilities, so a large area of land between the existing (1875) Newport yard site and Thornaby station was acquired in 1907 and authority given for construction of another new yard.

This new yard complex was designed for hump shunting by traditional methods (in contrast to the contemporary electro-pneumatic type of installation at Wath on the GC) and when opened on 14th December 1908 it took the name 'Erimus' from the motto of Middlesbrough ('We shall be'). The second diversion of the passenger lines took place under the 1908 Erimus scheme and a number of new bridges were built over the old course of the Tees, known

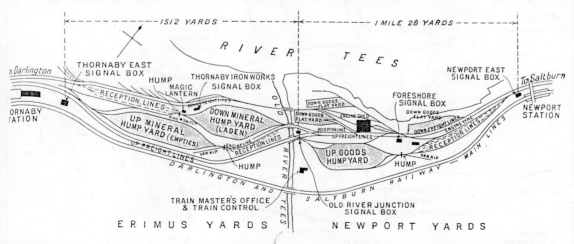

Drawing 4   NER layout of Erimus and Newport marshalling yards 1908 from an article published in the *NER Magazine* for April 1913.

(*Courtesy: Author's Collection*)

locally as the 'Old River', which flowed under the site. Following a further freight traffic working reorganisation during 1910/11 the final role of the four main yards became:

(Hump Yards) Erimus Laden Yard —
        Down Mineral traffic
        Erimus Empties Yard —
        Up Mineral empties
        Newport Up Goods —
        Up (outwards) Goods traffic
(Flat Yard) Newport Down Goods —
        Down (inwards) Goods traffic

Another feature associated with this busy period was the opening of Newport Control Office on 14th November 1910. Situated in the Yard Master's Office this pioneer traffic control installation undertook the general oversight, monitoring and deployment of resources necessary to ensure the most effective means of servicing the vast complex of works, docks and ironstone mines then to be found in the Tees-side and Cleveland district. It also regulated the flows of inwards mineral traffic to the area, ensured that collieries and works were supplied with empty wagons and arranged local freight train workings to ensure maximum efficiency.

The year 1913 marked the zenith of railway freight activity so far as the Shildon-Newport story goes. Indeed a few figures are necessary to demonstrate the growth of the North Eastern's mineral traffic over the period of time covered in this chapter:

NER Volume of Mineral Traffic Carried

Year	Coal and Coke Tons	Lime and Limestone Tons	Ironstone Tons	Total Tons
1870	15,058,598	1,177,498	3,816,772	20,052,868
1880	21,689,915	1,630,683	5,785,724	29,106,322
1890	26,266,510	2,126,611	4,728,185	33,121,306
1900	33,316,191	2,213,779	5,019,268	40,549,238
1910	40,390,130	2,499,341	6,025,431	48,914,902

Output of Durham Coalfield

Year	Tons
1870	21,773,275
1880	28,063,346
1890	30,265,241
1900	34,800,719
1910	39,431,598

There is little doubt that the heavy traffic levels experienced from 1910 onwards set the scene for the electrification which followed, but in the event 1913 proved to be the end of an era in more ways than one. World War I resulted in dramatic changes and afterwards things were never quite the same again. The prosperous period of heavy industrial growth had, alas, run its course and there could be no return to the boom days of 1913. Then came the Railways Act of 1921 which resulted in the 1923 groupings, thus the North Eastern Railway lost its independence (though fortunately not its character!) and from 1st January 1923 it became part of the newly formed LNER.

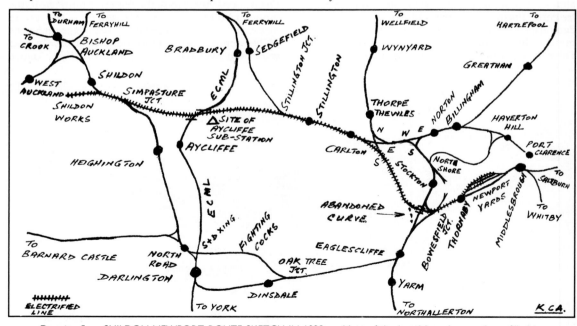

Drawing 5   SHILDON-NEWPORT ROUTE SKETCH IN 1923 — Most of the 'gaps' have by now been filled in.

3. THE ELECTRIFICATION ERA 1913-1935

The North Eastern was in the forefront amongst pre-grouping main line companies to become involved in electrification. As far back as 1904 (under the auspices of the then General Manager Sir George Gibb), the North Eastern successfully electrified their North Tyneside suburban services in an attempt to combat increasing competition from the expanding electric tramway system in and around Newcastle. Also in 1904 the Newcastle Quayside branch was electrified; this being a steeply graded sharply curved freight line about one mile in length, situated mostly in tunnel and extremely difficult to work with steam locomotives.

Much of the credit for this earlier Tyneside electrification belongs to Charles Merz, soon to become a leading name in the contemporary electrical world and co-founder of the firm of consulting engineers Merz and McLellan, whose activities became synonymous with NER electrification. Merz spared no effort to preach the electrification gospel and doubtless some of this initial enthusiasm rubbed off on to Vincent Raven. Raven was a visionary — a progressive and far-seeing engineer who in some respects (electrification being one of them) could be looked upon as being a man before his time.

In 1910 Raven became Chief Mechanical Engineer of the NER and in 1911 Sir Alexander Kaye Butterworth — the General Manager who succeeded Sir George Gibb — officially appointed Messrs Merz & McLellan as the company's consulting engineers, giving them a remit to report upon railway electrification with particular reference to the North Eastern's main routes. (In modern parlance, a feasibility study!)

Raven and Merz went over to the USA shortly afterwards to view at first hand the effects of electrification upon several North American railroads, some of which had been actively involved with electric traction since the early 1900s. The outcome of this trip across the Atlantic was that the NER Board of Directors decided to embark upon a 'pilot scheme' — thus Shildon-Newport emerged as the route chosen for evaluation and trial. This particular choice was largely determined by the Shildon-Newport's inbuilt advantage of being relatively self-contained, of possessing a stable heavy mineral traffic flow between two well defined points (Shildon Yard and Erimus) where electrification would not

unduly impinge upon conventional steam operation, and passenger services did not necessarily become involved. Furthermore, this trial scheme could provide meaningful practical experience yet pay its way by effecting a significant cost reduction in working the traffic. Actual work on providing the electrification infrastructure started on 16th June 1913.

The techniques of electricity generation had in the first decade of this century become well established in the North East, thus an inherent advantage of both the North Tyneside Suburban and the proposed Shildon-Newport schemes was the ready availability of electrical energy at a reasonable price, which in turn saved the NER the heavy capital expenditure associated with provision of dedicated power station plant. It was decided to adopt the high tension direct current system, power being transmitted to the locomotives through overhead contact wires at 1500 volts DC supplied from two purpose built rotary converter sub-stations — one at Aycliffe and the other at Erimus (Middlesbrough). Aycliffe sub-station could easily be seen from main line passenger trains between Darlington and Newcastle. It was situated east of the main line adjacent to the bridge where the Simpasture Branch crossed over the top, about a mile north of Aycliffe station.

The overhead contact wires for much of the route consisted of two hard drawn copper conductors (ie double wires) but on certain downhill stretches of line and portions of sidings where power loadings were not so heavy, only a single contact wire was used. The overhead contact wires themselves were supported by a solid steel auxiliary wire to which they were attached by sliding clips. This auxiliary catenary was in turn suspended from the main stranded steel catenary by means of steel wire droppers. The main steel catenary wire was supported from the steel structures by means of special insulators — double insulation was used throughout.

The normal spacing between the steel structures was originally around 300 feet but on curves and sidings they were placed at lesser intervals dependent upon prevailing conditions. Subsequently it was found in practice that high winds tended to whip the wires off locomotive pantographs, so some intermediate gantries had to be inserted at exposed

Fig 6   Aycliffe sub-station when new in 1914.   *(Courtesy: Railway Gazette)*

Fig 7   Stillington Junction pre-electrification work in progress c1914.   *(Courtesy: K.L. Taylor collection)*

Fig 8   Electrification Masts (1) — looking westwards to Simpasture Junction 1914. *(Courtesy: Railway Gazette)*

Fig 9   Electrification Masts (2) — looking westwards from Carlton (Redmarshall) station 1914.
(Courtesy: Railway Gazette)

locations. (Thereafter the British Standard became 210-220 feet.) Normal height of the copper contact wire from rail level was 16ft 6ins but at level crossings this was increased to 18ft 6ins, and under some of the low bridges the height was reduced to a minimum of about 13ft 8ins. Each steel structure carried a pair of insulated steadying arms. These steadying arms were pivoted in all directions, and were attached to the contact wires by means of clips, their purpose being to fix the position of the contact wires relatively to the track. The contact wires were staggered in the usual way to prevent undue wearing of the pantographs on the electric locomotives.

Generally, the usual type of steel structure carrying the wires consisted of two steel masts and a cross girder, each of these being made up of two channels with flat steel bracing. On curves a centre strut steadied by steel tie rods was added with independent 'pull off' masts for very sharp curvature. In certain instances, eg multiple tracking, cantilever construction was adopted. In order to limit as far as possible the sag of the contact wires due to temperature variation, automatic tensioning was adopted — the tensioning points were approximately 1,100 yards apart. On some of the sidings, where only slow speed shunting operations were carried out and power demands on the locomotives were not so heavy as when running a train, a single contact wire was strung over each track using ordinary tramway span wire construction. At marshalling yard and reception sidings which were not equipped throughout and at which it was only necessary for limited overhead construction to permit of the electric locomotives entering to attach or detach their load, the wires were terminated at a sufficient distance. Danger boards were fitted beyond which electric locomotives should not pass, but if by any chance over-running did occur, the terminal construction was such that no damage would be done to the pantographs or overhead line equipment.

When passing under low overbridges it was possible in some cases to carry the main catenary wire through the bridge, but at others it was necessary to anchor it off. In these cases, in order to obtain the necessary clearance, the contact wires, together with the auxiliary catenary were brought towards the centre of the bridge so that contact was made towards the extreme edge of the pantograph. In order to prevent the other edge of the pantograph from striking the bridge a guard wire was fitted.

Fig 10   Electrification Masts (3) — looking from Bowesfield West towards Bowesfield. Note abandoned Hartburn West Curve to right of picture. By 1914 the curve was a siding serving a local brickyard.
(Courtesy: Railway Gazette)

Fig 11   Electrification Masts (4) — looking at the Castle Eden Branch curving away to the right from Bowesfield Junction 1914.
(Courtesy: Railway Gazette)

This guard wire was anchored off to the structures on either side of the bridge and was only live while a locomotive was actually passing underneath. Wooden guards were placed above the parapets of overbridges to avoid injury or electric shock to persons who might be tempted to investigate too closely!

Section switches were erected as necessary so that sections of overhead line could be isolated for maintenance purposes and other engineering work. These switches were grouped together so they could be operated from conveniently located signal boxes, and remarkably enough they were manually worked from lever frames specially installed in purpose-built extensions to some (but not all) signal boxes. The isolation arrangements were co-ordinated on behalf of the Engineering Departments by the Traffic Control Office at Newport and the signalmen operated their sectioning switch levers as and when instructed by Control.

The two sub-stations on the system were supplied with three-phase current from the interconnected mains system of the North East Coast Power Companies through the Cleveland and Durham Electric Power Company; Aycliffe was supplied with current at 20,000 volts AC through two overhead lines, and Erimus took power at 11,000 volts AC via underground cables connected with the electric mains in Middlesbrough. Aycliffe sub-station contained two 800 kw rotary sets, each set consisting of two 400 kw rotary converters in series. The rotary converters were built by the British Thomson-Houston Company Ltd, the transformers being of the British Westinghouse Company's make. At Erimus sub-station the equipment was much the same except that one of the converters was of 1200 kw capacity. Both sub-stations did substantially the same job, namely to convert the mains electricity supply, in this case three phase high tension AC to the 1500 volts DC needed to run the trains. The fleet of 10 electric locomotives (numbered 3-12 inclusive, because Nos 1 and 2 were the Newcastle Quayside Branch locomotives) was designed and built at Darlington North Road Works, the electrical equipment being supplied and fitted by Siemens Bros Dynamo Works Ltd, Stafford. They weighed just over 74 tons each and were designed with an optimum haulage capacity of 1400 tons at a normal speed of 25 mph on level track in mind, plus the capacity to start a train of this tonnage on a 1 in 300 rising gradient.

These machines were of the Bo-Bo type (wheel

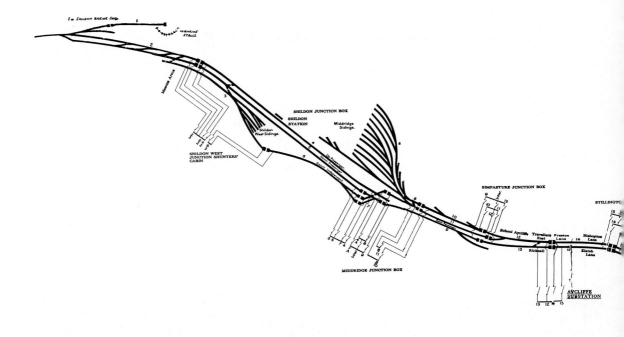

Drawing 6   NER SHILDON-NEWPORT electrification sectioning plan, 1915.   *(Courtesy: K. Hoole Collection)*

arrangement 0-4+4-0) and in reality were two separate electric motive power units. The body design (positioned on a single chassis) incorporated a centre cab which carried two pantographs, or bow collectors in old technical language. These were raised and maintained in contact position with the overhead line by compressed air; a novel safety feature being that the removable handle of the compressed air cock formed the key to the engine room doors, thus access to the electrical gear could only be effected when the compressed air cock handle was in the 'exhaust' position (ie with the pantograph down and the locomotive immobilised).

Two master controllers were fitted in the cab — one at each end — and another feature of note (in addition to the Westinghouse air brake) was an air controlled sanding device. The traction equipment for each locomotive consisted of four totally enclosed motors, two to each bogie, which drove the axles through single reduction twin gearing. The pair of motors on each bogie (each wound for 750 volts) were connected permanently in series and controlled on the series parallel system. A motor driven air compressor was fitted in each locomotive cab to supply air for the Westinghouse brake equipment, the air sanders, raising the pantographs and even to blow the air whistle! An emergency hand pump was provided so that the pantographs could be raised at

the start of work if no pressure was available in the reservoir, but in the event of a failure to maintain correct air pressure during the journey the pantographs were automatically lowered. The air cylinders raised the pantographs through springs which maintained an even pressure against the live contact wire notwithstanding variations in its height.

One of the existing engine sheds at Shildon was specially adapted to house the ten strong electric fleet. An automatic circuit breaker was provided controlling the whole of the shed equipment, and each engine stall was controlled by an independent isolating and earthing switch so that work could be carried out with safety on locomotive roofs and superstructures without interfering with the operation of other machines in adjacent stalls.

The original overhead line equipment contractors were Siemens-Schuckert but due to the outbreak of war in 1914 this company was obliged to withdraw and the work was finished by the British Insulated & Helsby Cable Company Ltd (a predecessor of British Insulated Callenders Construction Company Ltd). The main agreement dated 9th May 1913 between the NER and Siemens Bros Dynamo Works Ltd stipulated completion (to the satisfaction of the NER engineers and subject to Board of Trade inspection) within 18 months, and while work actually commenced on 16th June 1913, the onset of World

War I in 1914 radically affected the scheme's progress. The fact that work advanced far enough to permit a partial introduction of electric operation by 1st July 1915 was in itself a tribute to the dedication and initiative shown by the NER's civil and mechanical engineering staff left to carry the scheme through after most of the original contractor's personnel had returned to Germany.

Raven himself was seconded to essential government service in September 1915 and became Chief Superintendent of Woolwich Arsenal. He did not return to the NER until 1919. During his enforced absence the reins were held by A.C. Stamer to whom had fallen the task of implementing the Shildon-Newport electrification project.

subject to a length limit of equal to 70 wagons for Erimus Down Receptions. In the reverse direction the permitted empty loading was 563 tons or a maximum of 90 empty wagons.

During the first two or three years of the electrification era, much valuable experience was gained of a completely new and previously untried situation. Following Sir Vincent Raven's return to the North Eastern fold in 1919 (he had been awarded the KBE in 1917), he was instrumental in paving the way to even greater things — namely the ambitious York-Newcastle main line electrification scheme. No one in those euphoric days immediately following the end of World War I could conceivably have foreseen the harsh financial and economic

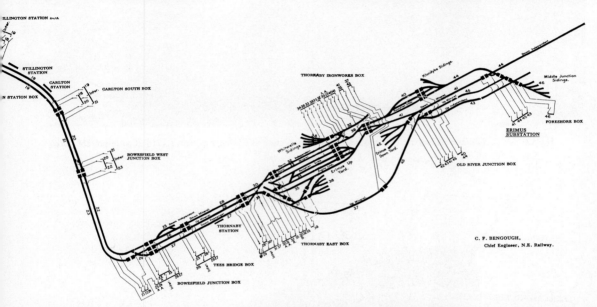

Introduction of electric working was of necessity staged viz:

1. Middridge-Bowesfield West   1st July 1915
2. Shildon-Middridge   30th October 1915
3. Bowesfield West-Erimus   22nd November 1915
4. Erimus-Newport East   10th January 1916

Initially a night service only was operated in order to allow for daytime possessions to accelerate completion. For this night shift working three electric locomotives between them made a total of eight round trips and the train loadings were at first limited to those applicable to steam, which for this route were well within the rated capacity of the new machines. Official electric train loadings published in June 1917 stipulated a maximum tonnage of 980 tons for mineral or concentrated goods loads (which could be increased by 15% if in 20T wagons),

problems with which this country, its heavy industries and its railway system would be faced during the twenties. On the one hand, impressed by the undoubted technical success of the Shildon-Newport electric locomotives — which fully matched up to their designed expectations — and spurred on by a deep conviction as to the benefits of electrifying the York-Newcastle main line, Raven pushed forward with the submission of an impressive project. He also sought initial authority to proceed with the design and building of a large main line electric passenger locomotive.

On the other side of the coin there was the stark fact that in order to achieve main line electrification one must first of all be prepared to embark upon significant capital expenditure, and what may have held good in the prosperous days of 1913 was not

Fig. 12   Unidentified Electric Locomotive under construction at Darlington Works 1914. *(Courtesy: NRM, York)*

Fig. 13   Electric Locomotive No 3 on trial run *c*1915 passing Preston Lane crossing on its way back to Shildon.
(Courtesy: K.L. Taylor collection)

Fig. 14   Shildon Shed showing Electric Locomotives Nos 3, 5, 7, 8 and 9 on 30th June 1927.
(Courtesy: H.G.W. Household)

Fig. 15   The inaugural Shildon-Newport electrically hauled mineral train leaving the Middridge end of Shildon
Yard on 1st July 1915. (Electric Locomotive No 3.) Note the overbridge in the background is still there
but the row of cottages has disappeared.   *(Courtesy: Railway Gazette)*

necessarily valid in the vastly changed economic climate some 6 to 7 years later. Suffice it to say (because York-Newcastle electrification is really another story) that the NER Directors, increasingly worried at the widely fluctuating interest rates on the money market, stalled at the daunting prospect of raising a vast capital sum in the prevailing financial situation. Despite the inherent advantages of electrification so ably and rightly expounded by Raven, there were a couple of spectres around that would not go away and they ultimately decided the fate of his vision for an electric main line. These were the serious decline from 1920 onwards of the very traffic which had provided the original justification for electrifying Shildon-Newport, and just around the corner was the grouping of 1923.

In retrospect the LNER has sometimes been blamed for not proceeding with Raven's main line electrification but this is rather unfair; it was the economic and industrial decline of the 1920s, not the LNER which killed off the scheme.

Raven was, however, successful with his bid for an electric passenger locomotive — hence the famous No 13, a 4-6-4 type, which appeared in 1922 and apart from test runs on the Shildon-Newport line did little or no revenue earning work. Nevertheless, the

various tests conducted during 1921 with and without the dynamometer car, proved the superiority of electric traction and from 29th November 1922 the permitted mineral loadings were increased to make provision for conveyance of 70 'mixed' loaded wagons with a maximum weight of 1400 tons. In his heyday, Sir Vincent Raven claimed (with justification!) that five electrics were doing the work of thirteen steam locomotives and there can be no doubt that the theoretical advantages of electric over steam were put to the test, and proved in practice on the Shildon-Newport line.

Then almost in the final hours of the North Eastern's separate existence an accident occurred, which for a time threw doubts upon the manner in which heavy trains were handled on falling gradients. At about 6.50 am on 29th December 1922 a loaded mineral train hauled by electric No 6 while travelling on the down mineral line between Stillington and Carlton (Redmarshall), overran the down home signal at Carlton (Redmarshall) Station Box and collided with a steam hauled train of empties which was being crossed from the up Passenger Line to up Mineral Line ahead of it. Damage to rolling stock and permanent way was significant though fortunately neither serious injuries nor damage to the

Fig 16   Electric Locomotive No 8 hauling a train of NER coke wagons approaching Bowesfield West c1922.
(Courtesy: R. Sowler)

Fig. 17   Electric Locomotive No 11 near School Aycliffe crossing with loaded train for Newport, 14th May 1923.

(Courtesy: W. Rogerson)

overhead line equipment occurred as a result. The accident was investigated by Major G.M. Hall of the newly formed Ministry of Transport (Board of Trade pre-1919) and in his report dated 22nd February 1923 (the LNER had come into being by then) he went into great detail about the methods used for computation of loads, the techniques for handling heavy trains on falling gradients and the inherent danger (applicable even more so today) which arises when a driver is not in possession of full and accurate data regarding the composition and weight of his train. In this instance the Inspecting Officer concluded that the train consisting of 28×20T wagons and 41×10T wagons (all loaded) with a total gross weight of 1396 tons (within 4 tons of the authorised limit), became overpowered while travelling down the long 1 in 230 falling gradient from Stillington to Carlton and he called into question the driver's braking technique which resulted from an apparent — though not admitted — misunderstanding and failure of communication between the Yard Inspector at Shildon, the guard, the fireman (described as a 'helper'!) and the driver. In fact the Inspecting Officer concluded that while responsibility for the accident was largely attribut-

able to the driver, and to a lesser degree his 'helper', urgent steps needed to be taken to ensure that henceforth definite and accurate information should be handed to the driver, preferably in writing, which could be looked upon as the forerunner of the present day piece of paper known as the 'driver's slip' or more accurately 'train consist'. Comments were also forthcoming about the manner in which the train loadings were computed, and the permissive block system in force over this particular stretch of line, though the braking system on the electric locomotive itself escaped criticism.

In the event, the lessons learned from this, the one serious accident which had occurred since the electrification was introduced just a few years previously proved to be somewhat academic. By the mid-1920s the effects of economic decline had begun to be felt in this part of the world and the traffic volume fell rapidly.

During the early 1930s the LNER was really feeling the pinch as the gap between revenue and working expenses widened. The original cost of the Shildon-Newport electrification was estimated at 1913 prices to be £150,000 (of which £50,000 was for locomotives), though the actual cost — at World

War I prices — was said to be more like £200,000. The ton-mileage statistics for this section which had peaked to an estimated 52 million for 1913, dipped to 40 million tons in 1917 and decreased alarmingly to around 7 million tons in 1930, were cause enough for concern. The accountants of the day reckoned that the return on expenditure never exceeded 5% even at best, and had rapidly diminished since 1920, the last 'normal' year for the North Eastern's coal carryings. Another background slant to the problem was that the LNER and NESCO (who had purchased the Cleveland and Durham power network in 1917) were having negotiations about the comparative level of charges raised for electricity on the Tyneside Suburban and Shildon-Newport lines. The LNER maintained that the charges around Newcastle were too high and were seeking a reduction. NESCO (Newcastle upon Tyne Electric Supply Company), on the other hand said that their Shildon-Newport charges were unduly low and pressed for an increase to bring their supplies for the Aycliffe and Erimus sub-stations up to a more remunerative level.

Clearly an impasse of this nature caused the LNER to think seriously about their Shildon-Newport operation and an exercise conducted in 1933 concluded that reversion to steam haulage would produce significant savings. It must also be remembered that large numbers of steam locomotives were then in store due to the depressed state of business. Yet another feature was that the agreement for power supply would run out in 1937 and it had been found both practicable and economical to work the reduced amount of traffic direct from collieries to steelworks and so on, enabling further savings to be made in marshalling costs.

Thus the writing was on the wall for the Shildon-Newport scheme; its initial technical success was by now showing every sign of becoming a commercial disaster. Electric train operations by 1933-34 were already very much reduced and it was also becoming evident that despite the locomotives being in good condition much of the overhead line equipment would soon be due for renewal. During 1934 the LNER grasped the nettle and NESCO were given notice that the power supply agreement dated 14th February 1913 would be terminated with effect from 1st January 1935. Electric operation ceased after 31st December 1934, and sadly the electrification era came to an end.

Concurrently with the reversion to steam haulage, Shildon Yard, which had already been reduced to one shift by 1932, was closed with effect from 7th January 1935. (An internal LNER memo quoted it only having a throughput of one seventh of the 1913 traffic volume.) The electric locomotives were put into store at Darlington and following a major reorganisation of motive power affairs in South West Durham as from 8th July 1935, Shildon shed too was closed.

Sir Vincent Raven died on 14th February 1934, shortly before the premature demise of his first major electrification venture, and at least it is gratifying to know that by 1991 we can expect to see electric trains running on the York-Newcastle main line — not quite the same type of trains or infrastructure that Raven would have designed, but thanks in no small measure to his pioneering efforts 70 years ago.

Fig 18 Electric Locomotive No 13 in 'workshops grey' livery hauling westbound test train on the Simpasture Branch 4th June 1922. The rear of the train has just cleared the bridge carrying the Shildon-Newport route over the ECML. *(Courtesy: NRM, York)*

Fig 19   Electric Locomotive No 13 in LNER green livery at Darlington Works painted in readiness for the Centenary procession 2nd July 1925.   *(Courtesy: NRM, York)*

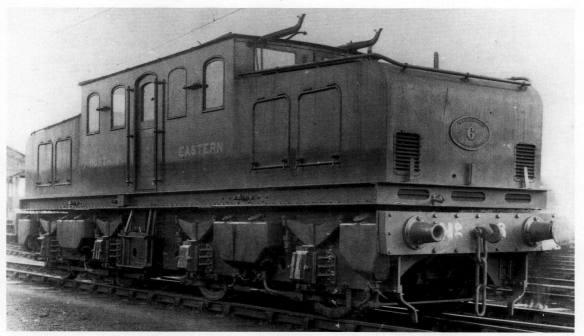

Fig. 20   Electric Locomotive No 6 in trouble, after having lost a buffer in the Carlton accident on 29th December 1922 (taken at Darlington Works).   *(Courtesy: K.L. Taylor collection)*

Fig. 21   Electric Locomotive No 6 leaving Middridge sidings at Shildon bound for Newport 30th June 1927.
(Courtesy: H.G.W. Household)

Fig. 22   Electric Locomotive No 10 in Shildon Yard on 30th June 1927.   *(Courtesy: H.G.W. Household)*

4. RECESSION AND WORLD WAR II

The trade recession and resultant slump which followed the end of World War I seriously affected the railways of South West Durham and Tees-side. Times were bad in the North East during the 1920s and 30s; heavy industry and coal mining were in a depressed state and this rubbed off on the railways' freight business in no uncertain manner. The situation reached by the early 1930s was in fact the very reverse of the expansionist era that had preceded World War I. A period of retrenchment and contraction set in and, apart from a revival during World War II, this downward trend continued culminating in the virtual demise of the Shildon-Newport route as such during the 1960s.

Dismantling and demolition of the overhead electrification structures, which started in 1935, continued during 1936/37, though the derelict and ruined buildings which had housed the two electric sub-stations at Aycliffe and Erimus remained standing as gaunt reminders to Sir Vincent Raven's memory for many years afterwards. The Aycliffe ruins disappeared shortly after the time that the new A1(M) main road was being constructed during the 1960s, though the site upon which the sub-station was built can still be located adjacent to the Blacksmith's Arms public house, situated just off a minor road called Ricknall Lane which runs between the A167 near Newton Aycliffe and Great Stainton. The Erimus site at Oswald Terrace, Middlesbrough finally vanished around 1959/1960 when a start was made on constructing the new Tees Yard.

The roundhouse at Shildon which had been purposely adapted to house the electric locomotive fleet was eventually taken over by the Wagon Works in 1938, the electrics having by then been transferred to Darlington North Road and put into store. When Shildon shed was closed from 8th July 1935 (along with another shed at Wear Valley Junction) the remaining steam locomotives and crews were transferred to nearby West Auckland (which itself had been closed between 13th April 1931 and 8th July 1935 due to the depressed state of traffic).

Shildon marshalling yard closed down from 7th January 1935, having been reduced to one shift working only since 1932, and contemporary reports cited the throughput as having dropped to one seventh of the 1913 traffic level. However, it must be said that apart from the trade recession the decline of the South West Durham coalfield became inevitable as the mining activity in County Durham tended to

Fig 23   NER class T 0-8-0 (Q5) 2123 (BR 63257) heading eastwards c1937 near School Aycliffe crossing.
(Note the redundant electrification structures, minus overhead wires.)   *(Courtesy: J.W. Armstrong)*

Fig 24   Ruins of Aycliffe sub-station looking east 7th March 1964.   *(Courtesy: R. Goad)*

move progressively towards the coast. Most of the newer twentieth century pits being sunk on or near the coast (such as those around Seaham) had coal faces which actually extended under the sea bed, in some cases for several miles. Another factor which altered the traditional traffic flows was the emergence during the 1920s of a radically changed mineral leading pattern in the North East involving more block train loads direct from the larger collieries to major industrial consumers, giving better transit times and improved utilisation of resources (locomotives, rolling stock and train crews) by avoiding the marshalling yards at Shildon and Newport. One effect of these revised workings was a significant reduction in traffic volume passing via the electrified route, and yet another tragedy of this same period was the closure of North Stockton marshalling yard from 9th June 1930.

Many of Tees-side's iron and steel works, and most of its ship yards, went out of business during the slump and others were rationalised in the various takeovers and mergers of the day which eventually left Messrs Dorman Long and the South Durham Steel and Iron Company as the two main survivors. In fact probably the only bright spot in an otherwise gloomy picture of industrial Tees-side in the 1930s was ICI Billingham (the successor to the Synthetic Ammonia & Nitrate Company which had established itself at Billingham towards the end of World War I). Contrary to the prevailing business trends of the day, ICI provided much needed employment and generated large quantities of rail traffic — which somehow helped to make the atmospheric pollution seem worthwhile!

By way of contrast to the developments at Erimus and Newport yards during the first decade of this century, the early 1930s resulted in contractions as

the wagon throughput fell. The 'Down Goods' yard at Newport was closed in 1931, all inwards shunting/marshalling activities then being concentrated at the Erimus 'Down Mineral' yard, and this was followed in 1936 by a major reorganisation from which three main yards emerged and most of the residual smaller yards and groups of sidings at Newport were closed. Newport Up Goods Yard (known as G1) became No 1 Up Yard — dealing with predominantly South traffic — while Erimus empties yard became No 2 Up Yard dealing mainly with wagons for North and West destinations. Erimus laden yard became Newport No 1 Down Yard (known as 'Down Mineral') and allied to this rationalisation was a combination of the District Operating Superintendent's offices at Middlesbrough and Darlington. These were merged into a new Darlington District (and enlarged Control Office) from June 1936. The proud title 'Erimus' was officially dropped from railway usage in 1936, the whole yard henceforth being called 'Newport' (until the name changed again to Tees Yard in 1962/1963). Surplus locomotives were 'tallowed down', their internal mechanism and other moving parts being smothered in grease and even leather caps were fitted over chimneys to keep out the rain!

Other cost cutting measures during this period involved withdrawal of the Stockton-Wellfield passenger service from 2nd November 1931 while on the Stockton-Ferryhill branch steam Sentinel Cars were introduced.

Towards the end of 1937 industrial activities on Tees-side began to show signs of recovery and everyone hoped that the end of the recession was near. As the storm clouds of war gathered on the horizon during 1938/39 things began to regain momentum; it became particularly noticeable that stored freight locomotives and wagons were gradually being returned to traffic. Even the Shildon-Newport route became relatively busy again, albeit without its electrics!

Both North Stockton and Shildon yards were reopened around the time that World War II commenced in 1939. Traffic levels soon showed a marked increase, and the occupational hazards of operating a railway during the blackout soon became painfully evident, especially so when work was interrupted by air raid warnings most nights from 1940 onwards. Congestion became inevitable, particularly at Newport Down Mineral Yard, and during the early 1940s it was not uncommon to see an almost continuous queue of freight trains most afternoons and evenings stood back on the Castle Eden Branch at Bowesfield, competing with other freight trains coming from the Eaglescliffe direction and Hartburn Curve, all waiting for a turn to join a similar queue on the Down Mineral Line at Thornaby East. The Thornaby queue waited for the next available empty reception line in Newport Down Mineral Yard and just as soon as one of the yard pilots had pushed a reception load over the hump another train moved forward from Thornaby

East to take its place. And so it went on for hours on end, while the signalmen at Bowesfield did their best to turn out through mineral loads for destinations east of Newport on to the Down Passenger Line as margins became available among the frequent passenger services. At times the whole scenario was rather like a game of chess — whose move next?

Actually the yard staff at Newport (and North Stockton too) did an absolutely marvellous job under what at times were almost impossible conditions, particularly in the dark and during ARP (air raid precaution) warnings; indeed it is a tribute to them, coupled with the dedication and resourcefulness of train crews, signalmen and controllers that Tees-side's heavy industries were kept supplied with ever increasing quantities of raw materials, not forgetting the supply of empty steel carrying wagons necessary for loading finished products. The increased throughput on the down side at Newport justified the eventual provision of two additional reception lines in 1944, which increased the number from five to seven.

Meanwhile Shildon Yard took on a new lease of life during World War II though the task it performed was completely different from that for

Fig. 25   An unidentified class J39 0-6-0 enters Shildon Up Yard Reception Lines with a mixed freight from the Bishop Auckland direction c1950s. (Shildon Works Branch to the left of picture and note vintage S&D type elevated points indicator still in use at the time.)   *(Courtesy: J.W. Armstrong)*

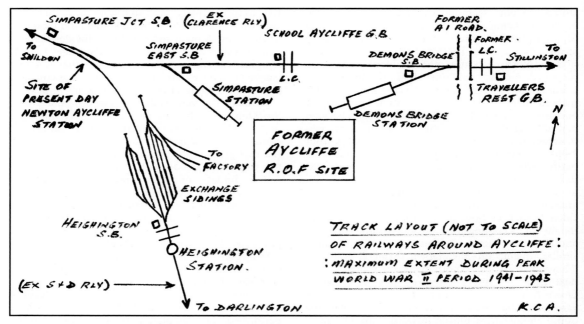

Drawing 7   ROYAL ORDNANCE FACTORY AYCLIFFE Track Layout during World War II. (Note Simpasture and
Demons Bridge passenger stations, and Exchange Sidings connected with Darlington-Bishop Auckland
line at Heighington.)
                                                                    (Courtesy: Author's Collection)

which it was originally designed. Instead of gathering
together the traffic originating from local collieries
and quarries for sorting and despatch, mainly to
Newport, it afforded relief to the various yards on
Tyneside while helping to minimise the effects of
wartime traffic congestion at Darlington and York
yards. Thus up (southbound) freight trains from
Low Fell, Heaton, Park Lane and the like were
diverted off the main line at Relly Mill (Durham)
and routed over the Bishop Auckland branch to
Shildon where they were terminated on the laden
yard Up Receptions. The locomotive was then
uncoupled and directed to the Simpasture end of the
yard to attach to a different southbound load (which
had previously been made up by gravitation
shunting) and worked forward to Darlington (for
crew change) en-route to York or beyond. Shildon
Yard in effect became a main line intermediate
staging point for the segregation and marshalling of
mixed South traffic to selected destinations beyond
York. Actually this wartime practice known as
'changing loads at Shildon' continued into the early
1960s; shunting was by gravitation, just as in the
pre-1935 closure days, and the yard operated on a
three shift basis throughout the war.

Probably the most spectacular development of the
World War II period relating to this story was the
establishment of Royal Ordnance Factory No 28 at
Aycliffe. The conveyance of large numbers of
passengers was envisaged and the LNER was asked
originally to provide facilities for dealing with some
30,000 munitions workers daily, though in the event
only around 12,000 daily had to be carried. Two
new spurs were built during 1941 each of which ran
off the (ex-Clarence Railway) Simpasture Branch to
a new passenger terminus situated within the factory
boundaries. Actually there were two passenger
termini; station 'A' at the western end became
known as 'Simpasture', and station 'B' at the eastern
end rejoiced in the unlikely name 'Demons Bridge'
— so called after the Demons Beck which flows
through the site. Heighington station on the (ex-
S&D) Darlington-Bishop Auckland line was also
enlarged to cope with additional passenger traffic.
Heighington took all the Darlington passengers,
Simpasture dealt with those who travelled to and
from the Bishop Auckland, Crook and Durham
locality, and Demons Bridge dealt with trains to and
from Tees-side, Hartlepool and the coastal mining
villages towards Seaham. Special trains ran just
before and immediately after shift changeover times
and were mainly hauled by the versatile A8 4-6-2T
locomotives, though Tees-side services were
frequently worked by A5s. Simpasture station had
two island platforms each 650ft long with four
platform lines and one engine release road, whereas

30

Fig 26   Simpasture East signal box (LNER wartime architecture) taken in 1949 prior to demolition and recovery of former factory station layout to right of picture.   *(Courtesy: R. Goad)*

Fig 27   Demons Bridge signal box (LNER wartime architecture) and former factory station layout to left, 15th August 1948.   *(Courtesy: J.W. Armstrong)*

LNER (NE AREA) WORKING TIMETABLE (WTT) MAY 4th 1942

DEMONS BRIDGE (From 4.5.42)

WEEKDAYS

FROM	ARRIVE	DEPART	TO
Hartlepool	6.6am	7.23am	Hartlepool
Grangetown	6.30am	7.38am	Grangetown
Hartlepool	2.1pm SX	3.23pm SX	Hartlepool
Saltburn	2.14pm SO ECS	3.38pm SO	Grangetown
West Hartlepool	2.30pm SO ECS	3.23pm SO	Hartlepool
Grangetown	2.30pm SX	3.38pm SX	Grangetown
Hartlepool	9.1pm SX	10.23pm SX	Hartlepool
Grangetown	9.30pm SX	10.38pm SX	Grangetown

SUNDAYS

FROM	ARRIVE	DEPART	TO
Hartlepool	2.1pm	2.35pm ECS	Hartlepool
Grangetown	2.30pm	3.0pm ECS	Saltburn
Hartlepool	9.1pm	10.23pm	Hartlepool
Grangetown	9.30pm	10.38pm	Grangetown

NOTES: (1) The Grangetown services ran ECS to and from Saltburn
(2) The Hartlepool services also called at Stillington

SIMPASTURE (From 4.5.42)

WEEKDAYS

FROM	ARRIVE	DEPART	TO
Durham	5.53am	7.20am	Durham
Tow Law	6.0am	7.28am	Tow Law
Durham	1.43pm SX)		
Tow Law	1.50pm SX)	3.20pm	Durham
Bishop Auckland	2.20pm SO ECS)	3.28pm	Tow Law
Leamside	2.35pm SO ECS)		
Durham	8.53pm SX	10.20pm SX	Durham
Tow Law	9.0pm SX	10.28pm SX	Tow Law

SUNDAYS

FROM	ARRIVE	DEPART	TO
Durham	1.43pm	2.20pm ECS	Leamside
Tow Law	1.50pm	3.20pm ECS	Bishop Auckland
Durham	8.53pm	10.20pm	Durham
Tow Law	9.0pm	10.28pm	Tow Law

Demons Bridge was larger with three island platforms (each 650ft in length) and two engine releases. Facilities were also provided at each station for watering and cleaning of locomotive fires during turn round periods. Both stations came into use early in 1942 (a precise opening date eludes the author) and the layouts were controlled by two new signal boxes called Simpasture East (opened 15th January 1942) and Demons Bridge (opened 12th December 1941).

The pattern of services which developed for the two wartime stations catered for nearly continuous shift working including weekends as shown in the table above.

The Simpasture station gained an extra train to and from Bishop Auckland for each of the three shifts when the WTT was next issued from 5th October 1942, and the Demons Bridge services which had been running ECS between Grangetown and Saltburn became passenger trains throughout. Activities at the factory were stepped up again during 1943/44; the 22nd May 1944 issue of the WTT showed an additional Demons Bridge service to and from Seaham, and the Simpasture-Durham services were by then running to and from Fencehouses.

At the peak during the 1944 winter service the arrivals and departures at the two wartime stations had settled down into the pattern shown opposite.

The WTT issue from 7th May 1945 catered for much the same service pattern, but not unexpectedly the munitions workers trains had disappeared from the 1st October 1945 WTT; the two stations by then having closed and the associated signal boxes switched out. (The only portion of the Simpasture Branch which did not encounter these wartime passenger trains was the short stretch between

WINTER (WTT) From OCTOBER 1944
DEMONS BRIDGE (From 5.10.44)
WEEKDAYS

FROM	ARRIVE	DEPART	DESTINATION
Hartlepool	6.14am	7.46am	Hartlepool
Seaham	6.22am	7.32am	Seaham
Saltburn	6.30am	7.40am	Saltburn
Hartlepool	2.14pm X	3.46pm	Hartlepool
Seaham	2.22pm X	3.32pm	Seaham
Saltburn	2.30pm X	3.40pm	Saltburn
Hartlepool	9.14pm SX	10.46pm SX	Hartlepool
Seaham	9.22pm SX	10.32pm SX	Seaham
Saltburn	9.30pm SX	10.40pm SX	Saltburn

X arrived ECS on Saturdays only.

SUNDAYS

Hartlepool	2.14pm	3.30pm ECS	West Hartlepool
Seaham	2.22pm	3.10pm ECS	Sunderland
Saltburn	2.30pm	3.0pm ECS	Saltburn
Hartlepool	9.14pm	10.46pm	Hartlepool
Seaham	9.22pm	10.32pm	Seaham
Saltburn	9.30pm	10.40pm	Saltburn

SIMPASTURE (From 5.10.44)
WEEKDAYS

FROM	ARRIVE	DEPART	TO
Bishop Auckland	6.15am	7.46am	Bishop Auckland
Tow Law	6.22am	7.32am	Tow Law
Fencehouses	6.30am	7.39am	Fencehouses
Bishop Auckland	2.15pm X	3.46pm	Bishop Auckland
Tow Law	2.22pm X	3.32pm	Tow Law
Fencehouses	2.30pm X	3.39pm	Fencehouses
Bishop Auckland	9.15pm SX	10.46pm SX	Bishop Auckland
Tow Law	9.22pm SX	10.32pm SX	Tow Law
Fencehouses	9.30pm SX	10.39pm SX	Fencehouses

X arrived ECS on Saturdays only.

SUNDAYS

Bishop Auckland	2.15pm	3.0pm ECS	Bishop Auckland
Tow Law	2.22pm	3.46pm ECS	Bishop Auckland
Fencehouses	2.30pm	3.10pm ECS	Penshaw
Bishop Auckland	9.15pm	10.46pm	Bishop Auckland
Tow Law	9.22pm	10.32pm	Tow Law
Fencehouses	9.30pm	10.39pm	Fencehouses

Demons Bridge and Simpasture East boxes which passed over the then School Aycliffe crossing — since replaced by St Cuthbert's Way bridge.)

For freight purposes Aycliffe ordnance factory was connected with the ex-S&D line at Heighington station where a sizeable sidings complex was laid down, along with an internal railway system operated by private locomotives.

Certainly World War II made the Shildon-Newport system very busy again. This was particularly noticeable between Bowesfield and Thornaby (still a busy stretch of line) where the four track section was intensively used by a mixture of freight and mineral trains to and from the Eaglescliffe, Stockton and Redmarshall directions together with frequent Darlington-Saltburn and Middlesbrough-Newcastle passenger services. Even over the 1885 'widened lines' between Redmarshall and Stillington North it was not uncommon for the Stillington North signalmen to deal with up to sixty trains on *each* of the early and late turns and thirty on night shift which takes some believing nowadays — a far cry from the mere handful of freight trains (as between Norton West and Ferryhill) which now pass this lonely and rather isolated place.

Fig 28   ROF9 No 7 0-4-0T *Peckett* at Newton Aycliffe Trading Estate 9th August 1960. (This locomotive worked on the ROF internal railway system — ROF No 9 actually became No 28, but the locomotives retained their original plates.)

(Courtesy: R. Sowler)

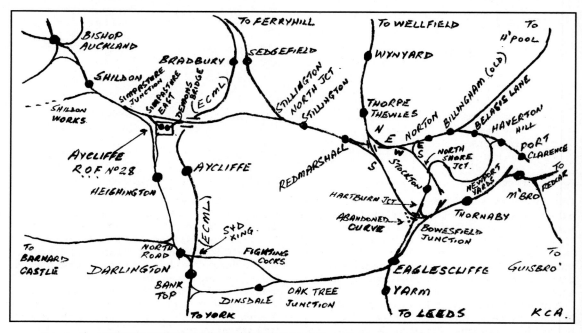

Drawing 8   SHILDON-NEWPORT ROUTE SKETCH IN 1942 — The maximum infrastructure in the area.

5. POST-WAR DECLINE — CLOSURES AND ABANDONMENTS

Soon after the war finished in 1945 and the munitions workers trains had ceased the new stations at Simpasture and Demons Bridge fell into disuse, along with their signal boxes, though the internal rail system within the Aycliffe factory (connected with the ex-S&D at Heighington) continued in use for a few more years to deal with freight traffic. The factory site itself was progressively redeveloped into a light industrial estate and by the early 1950s a completely new town known as Newton Aycliffe had sprung up.

The fortunes of the Durham coalfield changed rapidly after nationalisation of the mines; post-war development tended to concentrate upon the larger collieries situated nearer to the Durham coast which in turn caused demand to taper off for coal produced in the Shildon-Bishop Auckland area. The South West Durham coalfield eventually expired (apart from some opencast activities) and the rail traffic with it; even the sole remaining coke ovens at Randolph (near Evenwood) ceased to be rail connected during 1969.

Then the post-war rationalisation of the Tees-side iron and steel industry meant a gradual move eastwards from Middlesbrough towards newer sites established at Lackenby and Redcar, the emphasis henceforth being upon development of a smaller number of larger works incorporating the most modern steel manufacturing techniques. Eventually as this process was accelerated, iron and steel making disappeared altogether from the traditional 'Ironmasters District' of Middlesbrough and even the great Cargo Fleet works together with the massive plants around South Bank eventually succumbed. These various alterations drastically reduced the number of works and sidings formerly serviced by Newport Yards, and rail traffic for British Steel is now mainly concentrated upon the Lackenby Grids at Grangetown. Another new development was the Ore Terminal at Redcar, for which extensive rail facilities were installed in the early 1970s, but with the closure of Consett works and the run down of Workington, it has failed to produce anything like the planned volume of imported iron ore originally intended to pass by rail.

Similarly ICI Billingham, once a major consumer of Durham coal, underwent a major reorganisation — one effect of this being a change over to oil. Even the post-war development at ICI Wilton (located on the south bank of the Tees, which in 1951 involved construction of a new branch railway from Grangetown) ceased to receive coal by rail, though in more recent times the situation has been reversed and merry-go-round (MGR) coal trains now feed a purpose-built terminal.

These reductions in the basic work load of mineral haulage between South West Durham and the Tees, coupled with a completely different pattern of demand for rail freight movement on Tees-side involving more block trains of purpose-built high capacity wagons, heralded the inevitable run down of facilities and eventual disappearance of certain goods branches, leaving only the (ex-Clarence Railway) Norton West-Ferryhill section as the main survivor in the territory covered by this book.

Shildon Up Yard (the 'laden' yard) — reopened for World War II—continued performing its wartime role until the early 1960s, whereas Shildon Down Yard (the 'empties' yard) together with the adjacent Shildon West Sidings remained in being for many years to receive and grade wagons for repair ('cripples' in railway language) at Shildon Wagon Works.

The changed railway operations scene around Stockton and Middlesbrough during the 1950s resulted firstly in closure of Newport and Middlesbrough engine sheds and concentration upon a large new motive power depot at Thornaby, which was officially opened on 5th June 1958. This was closely followed by the closure of Stockton and Haverton Hill engine sheds in 1959. Construction of the new Thornaby shed was preceded by major track and signalling alterations, particularly at Thornaby East and Bowesfield where colour light signals replaced much of the traditional semaphore and mechanical signalling; also the passenger lines between Thornaby and Newport were diverted for the third and last time to make way for the new motive power depot together with the new marshalling yard still to come. The North Eastern Region's marshalling yard strategy which arose out of the 1955 British Railways Modernisation Plan (wagon load freight traffic was still buoyant in the mid-1950s) determined that one of the new modern yards was to be built on Tees-side, the preferred site being Newport. Thus from 1958 to 1963 a major upheaval took place which changed the face of Newport completely.

Fig 29   Class J39 0-6-0 64848 heads for Tees-side along the Simpasture Branch on 20th July 1959. (The overbridge in the background has since been filled in though one parapet still remains.)

(Courtesy: R. Sowler)

Fig 30   Simpasture Junction looking towards Shildon on 8th October 1967. By this time the Simpasture Branch connections had been lifted. (Note electrification extension added to signal box structure.)

(Courtesy: R. Goad)

Fig 31   The 'Parliamentary' junction site at Simpasture where the Clarence Railway originally joined the S&D. Class L1 2-6-4T 67763 heads a parcels train from Crook towards Darlington on 20th July 1959. (Note this is the site of the present day Newton Aycliffe station.)   *(Courtesy: R. Sowler)*

Fig 32   Another view of the original Simpasture Junction site on 4th April 1964 after the ex-Clarence line had been closed and used for surplus wagon storage purposes. (Note vintage S&D type platelayers hut.)
(Courtesy: R. Goad)

Tees Yard, as it became known from 1962, occupies a 200 acre site between Thornaby and Newport (see track layout pages 50/51). It is bounded on the north side by the River Tees and on the south by the Thornaby-Middlesbrough road (known locally as 'The Wilderness'). The passenger lines which originally ran through the centre of the yard site and were diverted southwards in 1875, and again in 1908, were finally diverted in two stages; the first stage (opened from Jan 12th 1958) skirted the new Thornaby shed and the second stage (opened 13th March 1960) continued parallel with 'The Wilderness' (and over the site of Erimus sub-station), having been delayed due to involvement with removal of some property situated near the 'Old River' — known as 'Erimus Cottages' — which although scheduled for demolition could only be achieved after re-housing of the residents was completed late in 1959.

Before the new yard could be laid out five new bridges had to be constructed across the 'Old River' to supplement the already existing structures dating from 1875 and 1908, and a quarter of a million tons of filling material was dropped to lift much of the site above its former waterlogged level.

Although called 'Tees Yard' from its *official* opening date of 21st May 1963, it was in fact two different (up and down) yards, being built with two distinctly separate hump control towers. The Down Yard was also provided with a secondary hump for the segregation of empty steel carrying wagons by type. Humping was assisted by all the sophisticated technological prerequisites which were to be found in modern marshalling yards of the 1960s 'big yard era', and the massive layout when complete totalled 153 sidings comprising 66 track miles. The Up Yard had 12 receptions, 40 sorting sidings and 12 departure lines, while the Down Yard had 12 reception lines, 40 main sorting sidings, 6 staging and 8 departure lines together with a subsidiary group of 10 secondary sorting sidings. Incorporated within the Down Yard Tower was a new power operated box, 'Tees Box', which became operative in its first stage from 12th August 1962. The new box overtook some of the new yard work (particularly on the up side) and permitted the closure of Newport

Fig 33   The scene at Thornaby East on 12th January 1958 during major track layout alterations and resignalling which involved diversion of the passenger lines around the then new Thornaby MPD site.

(Courtesy: British Rail)

Fig 34   Aerial view of the new Tees Yard under construction 5th October 1962 with Thornaby station in the
          foreground and Thornaby MPD to right.   *(Courtesy: British Rail)*

Fig 35   General view of the former Erimus Yards looking west from the newly constructed Tees Down Yard control tower, 19th January 1962.   *(Courtesy: British Rail)*

Fig 36   Tees Down Yard under construction looking east 9th July 1962. Note Old River signal box, together with the old course of the River Tees running under the site. The building on the right was the Yard Masters Office, Newport from where the original Newport Control operated between 1910 and 1930.

(Courtesy: British Rail)

Fig 37   Tees Down Yard control tower and power box under construction 16th April 1962. (Note both steam and diesel in evidence.)

(Courtesy: British Rail)

East box along with abandonment of the former goods line boxes called Old River and Foreshore, both of which had ceased to function because of the major track layout alterations then taking place on the down side. Final completion was achieved with effect from 12th May 1963 following the closure of Thornaby East box, and Tees Box presently covers the area between Bowesfield and Middlesbrough (former Middlesbrough West box). The signalling installation at Tees is of the 1960s style usual to the ex-North Eastern Region of BR, being an entrance-exit route relay interlocking provided with a 'NX' type push button console positioned in front of a large vertical illuminated display panel.

Designed with a total daily throughput capacity of 7,500 wagons in mind, Tees Yard did well on the few occasions during 1963 when it exceeded 4,000, and from 1964 onwards its failure to meet its planned expectations became painfully obvious — not that there was anything wrong with the yard, but the traffic volume just was not there! Britain's railways were at the time standing on the threshold of

what was later to become known as the 'Beeching Era', and in retrospect — admittedly with the benefit of hindsight — one cannot help but form the inescapable conclusion that Tees Yard (and some others like it) ought never to have been built on such a lavish scale.

The first casualty of the 1960s was the original 1833 Clarence Railway between Simpasture and Stillington North. The daily number of trains using the Simpasture Branch had by 1962 declined to a total of 10-15 in two shifts and there had been trouble on and off for several years caused by a very slow burning fire, apparently in old coal bearing measures under the formation around Simpasture Junction. This was at the point where the Clarence paralleled the S&D for a distance of 49 chains between the 'Parliamentary' junction (at the present Newton Aycliffe halt) and the eventual physical junction of the 1870s. Then the new A1(M) trunk road scheme came along, its construction involving a bridge under the Simpasture Branch between Aycliffe sub-station site and Preston Lane level

Fig 38   Travellers Rest signal box and former A1 road level crossing looking east in 1942. (The bracket signals were at that time worked by Demons Bridge box which had just recently been opened.)

(Courtesy: British Rail)

Fig 39   Ricknall Mill level crossing looking east 7th March 1964.   *(Courtesy: R. Goad)*

Fig 40   The ECML overbridge with an unidentified class 40 on an up main line train 7th March 1964.

(Courtesy: R. Goad)

Fig 41   Preston Lane level crossing looking east 7th March 1964.   *(Courtesy: R. Goad)*

crossing, which prompted a decision to close the line and so avoid bridging the proposed motorway. Also there was another road improvement scheme affecting Elstob Lane crossing, further along the branch towards Stillington, which again avoided construction of a new bridge.

After the cessation of freight train movements on Saturday 22nd June 1963 the Simpasture Branch was closed to all traffic and shortly afterwards severed at the then new A1(M) road construction works near Aycliffe, thus bringing to an end a line which created the first example of inter-railway competition. After 130 years the S&D had at last triumphed over the upstart Clarence, and Shildon-Newport traffic henceforth reverted to the old S&D route of 1825 via Fighting Cocks. By this time the original S&D line between Albert Hill (Darlington North Road) thence over the flat crossing with the east coast main line (ECML) and through Fighting Cocks to Oak Tree (where it joined the much later 1887 route from Darlington Bank Top which carries the present day Darlington-Saltburn passenger service) had been reduced to one shift, so it was necessary to extend it to two shifts to accommodate the erstwhile Simpasture Branch trains. It is also of interest to note that the Fighting Cocks Branch closed soon afterwards as a through route; from 21st May 1967 it was severed west of Messrs Paton

and Baldwin's factory siding near Darlington, thus the few remaining Shildon-Newport trains had to be diverted via Darlington Bank Top to rejoin the original S&D route at Oak Tree.

The quadruple track section (the 1885 widenings) between Redmarshall and Stillington North was the next candidate for rationalisation. Since the early 1960s the 'Mineral Lines' (by now called 'Goods Lines') had been temporarily closed to traffic and used for the storage of surplus wagons awaiting repair or condemnation. When the effects of the severe reduction in the wagon fleet began to be felt — yet another spin off from the 'Beeching Era' — this three miles or so of double track could accommodate something like 1250 stored wagons in total, the wagons being either condemned, awaiting condemnation, waiting to be graded, for repair, or just surplus to current requirements. Eventually, the unwanted wagons were removed (mostly to stand in North Stockton Yard which was closed in 1963 — for the second time) and on 18th October 1964 the mineral lines were broken in the vicinity of Stillington Station to facilitate construction of a road underbridge. The additional running lines were officially dispensed with as from 1st August 1965 following completion of signalling alterations at Stillington Station which also involved a realignment of tracks.

Fig 42   Elstob Lane level crossing looking west c1955 with class L1 2-6-4T 67765 on excursion train.
(Courtesy: J.W. Armstrong)

Fig 43   Bishopton Lane level crossing looking west c1963 shortly after closure of the line.
(Courtesy: Durham County Record Office)

Fig 44   Stillington North signal box (which was in the fork between the Simpasture Branch to the left and the
Ferryhill line to the right) with WD class 2-8-0 90445 on an enthusiasts brake-van tour c1964.
(Courtesy: Durham County Record Office)

Fig 45   A down main line express diverted via Stillington passing Stillington North c1955, hauled by class V2 2-6-2 60942. (Note the quadruple track, the mineral lines to right of picture being those which were electrified between 1915 and 1935.) *(Courtesy: J.W. Armstrong)*

Fig 46   The island platform station at Stillington c1964 prior to demolition. (The signal box and the tracks in the foreground still exist.) *(Courtesy: Durham County Record Office)*

Fig 47   Stillington Station signal box looking west on 5th July 1977. (No trace exists of the former island platform station.)
(Courtesy: R.J. Talbot)

Following closure of the Simpasture Branch in 1963, that part between Bishopton Lane and Elstob Lane level crossings was also temporarily used for wagon storage purposes (the formation had been broken at Elstob during December 1963 for road alterations and improvements) until the Simpasture Branch junction connections at Stillington North were removed on 15th August 1965.

The next line to go was the northern part of the Castle Eden Branch between the Redmarshall Junctions and Wingate South which closed to through traffic from 6th July 1966. Actually the Down (northbound) line between Redmarshall North and Wingate South had been closed to traffic for varying periods from 1945 to 1966, again for the storage of 'cripples' and other surplus wagons (mainly between Thorpe Thewles and Wynyard). When the Down line was out of use for wagon storage the branch effectively became 'one way' being worked in the up (southbound) direction only, this being different from other instances like the former NY&C branch between Picton and Ingleby where single line working by staff and ticket was introduced. Thus the empty mineral trains from Tees-side bound for collieries beyond Wellfield had to run via West Hartlepool and climb the steeply graded Hesleden bank to rejoin their intended route. In the reverse direction, of course, the loaded

mineral trains for Tees-side destinations could travel normally via the Wynyard Branch towards Redmarshall South and Bowesfield, (or Redmarshall North to East thence via Norton if for ICI Billingham), but as the formerly heavy line occupation through the West Hartlepool area had also declined somewhat, a decision was eventually taken to close the Wynyard route altogether. On 6th July 1966 the box at Wingate South was put out of use thus effectively severing this line as a through route, and the remaining stump from the Wellfield end was used by trains for Trimdon Grange Colliery until these ceased from 30th April 1969. So ended yet another of the North Eastern's expansionist lines of the 1870s, but worse was yet to come.

By now it had been found possible to work the remaining freight traffic still using the southern end of the 1877 Castle Eden Branch via Stockton and Norton West. Through traffic between Bowesfield and Redmarshall Station ceased as from 1st July 1967 though most of the trains had been diverted since January. The closure of Redmarshall Station Box followed on 25th November 1967, thus leaving only the line between Bowesfield and Redmarshall South for a little longer in order to gain access to stored wagons still left on the Wynyard Branch and on the now 'dead' line between Redmarshall South and Station. When eventually these were cleared,

Fig 48   Redmarshall Station signal box looking west c1964 and NER Class T2 (Q6) 0-8-0 2234 (BR 63391)
passing with a Thrislington (Ferryhill) to Cemetery North (Hartlepool) freight. *(Courtesy: R. Coulthard)*

Redmarshall South Box was closed as from 24th June 1968 and sadly the Castle Eden Branch was no more. The Castle Eden Branch junction at Bowesfield was put out of use during the weekend of 26th/27th October 1968 and track lifting was completed during 1969.

Thus ended the Shildon-Newport line as a separate entity; only that portion between the sites of the former junctions at Redmarshall and Stillington North remains to form an integral part of the Norton West-Ferryhill freight route which now carries a very low volume of freight traffic averaging something like one train per hour. It is still possible to see occasional block company trains of oil and chemicals plus the infrequent Tees-Tyne freights, though on Sundays the line often comes into its own as a diversionary route off the ECML when major engineering work takes place between Northallerton and Ferryhill — so one can even observe (and travel upon) HSTs if the right dates and times are chosen! At present the line is worked as one absolute block section, eleven miles long, between Norton West and Ferryhill with the only remaining intermediate signal box at Stillington Station normally switched out of circuit, being only opened as and when required for weekend main line diversions. There has, of course, been rumour and speculation about closure of this route, the residual freight traffic being diverted via Darlington, with complete or partial track singling as an alternative option. Nevertheless, while the line's inherent advantage as a diversionary route is currently being exploited in connection with ECML pre-electrification work, a question mark still seems to hang over its chances of survival after 1991.

At the Shildon end, most of the track in the marshalling yards was lifted by the mid-1970s and the sites cleared, and following the more recent demise of Shildon Wagon Works, which closed on 29th June 1984 even the original S&D route of 1825 over Masons Arms crossing and towards Brusselton has now been abandoned.

Fig 49　　Redmarshall (formerly Carlton) island platform station c1964 prior to demolition. (The remaining plain line double track now passes underneath the right hand portion of the road bridge to right of picture.)
(Courtesy: Durham County Record Office)

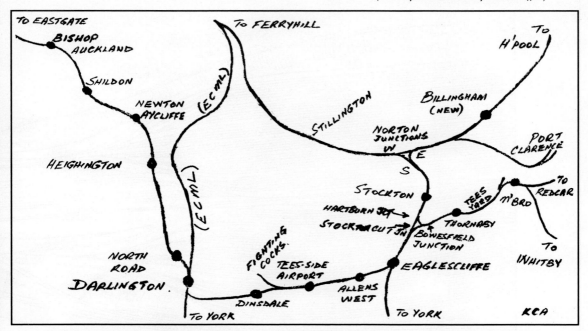

Drawing 10　SHILDON-NEWPORT ROUTE SKETCH IN 1989 — The present day very much scaled down position.

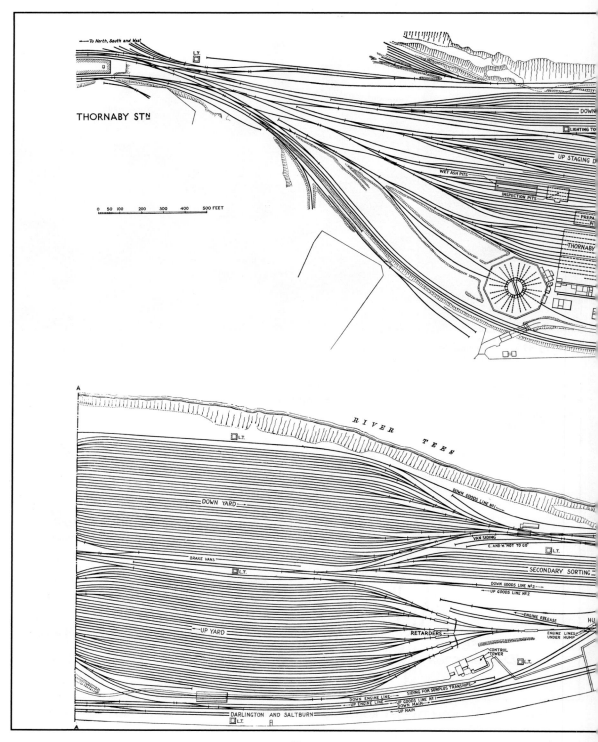

THORNABY STN

←—To North, South and West

L.T.

0 50 100   200   300   400   500 FEET

DOWN

LIGHTING TO

UP STAGING D

WET ASH PITS

INSPECTION PITS

PREPA
PI

THORNABY

A

RIVER   TEES

L.T.

DOWN YARD

DOWN GOODS LINE Nº1

VAN SIDING

C. AND W."NOT TO GO" L.T.

BRAKE VANS

L.T.

SECONDARY SORTING

DOWN GOODS LINE Nº2
UP GOODS LINE Nº2

ENGINE RELEASE

HU

←UP YARD

RETARDERS

ENGINE LINES
UNDER HUMP

CONTROL
TOWER   L.T.

SIDING FOR SURPLUS TRANSHIPS
DOWN ENGINE LINE
UP ENGINE LINE   UP GOODS LINE Nº1
                   DOWN MAIN

DARLINGTON AND SALTBURN
L.T.   UP MAIN

A

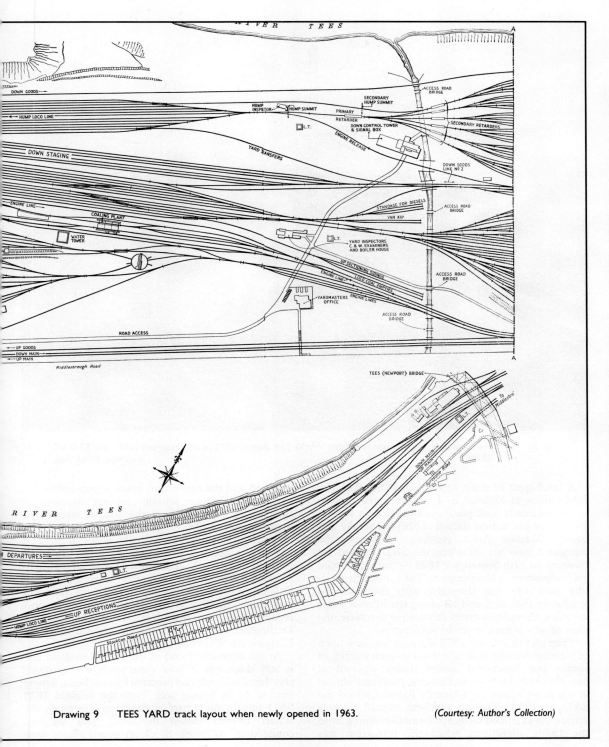

RIVER TEES

A

DOWN GOODS

HUMP LOCO LINE

HUMP INSPECTOR
HUMP SUMMIT

SECONDARY
HUMP SUMMIT

ACCESS ROAD
BRIDGE

PRIMARY
RETARDER

SECONDARY RETARDERS

L.T.

DOWN CONTROL TOWER
& SIGNAL BOX

DOWN STAGING

YARD TRANSFERS

ENGINE RELEASE

DOWN GOODS
LINE Nº 2

ENGINE LINE

COALING PLANT

WATER
TOWER

STANDAGE FOR DIESELS

ACCESS ROAD
BRIDGE

VAN KIP

L.T.

YARD INSPECTORS
C. & W. EXAMINERS
AND BOILER HOUSE

UP SECTIONING SIDINGS

ACCESS ROAD
BRIDGE

ENGINE LINE

LOCO COAL EMPTIES

ENGINE LINES

YARDMASTERS
OFFICE

ROAD ACCESS

ACCESS ROAD
BRIDGE

UP GOODS
DOWN MAIN
UP MAIN

A

Middlesbrough Road

TEES (NEWPORT) BRIDGE

To
Middlesbro

L.T.

DOWN MAIN
UP MAIN

Tyresene Road

RIVER TEES

DEPARTURES

L.T.

UP RECEPTIONS

HUMP LOCO LINE

Stockton Road

Drawing 9   TEES YARD track layout when newly opened in 1963.   (Courtesy: Author's Collection)

51

Fig. 50   Pre-Cavalcade line up outside Shildon Works 31st August 1975 (note preserved NER class T2 0-8-0 2238).

(Courtesy: British Rail)

A brief spell of glory accompanied the Rail 150 celebrations at Shildon in 1975 when the famous steam cavalcade took place on Sunday 31st August 1975. The procession started at Shildon Works and passed Masons Arms crossing — where the inaugural train set off when the S&D opened for business on 27th September 1825 — then proceeded via Simpasture to Heighington. The former marshalling yard site was thronged with thousands of spectators that day, and all along the lineside large crowds gathered to witness this unique spectacle, the likes of which may never be seen again.

Then on 9th January 1978 the post-war new town of Newton Aycliffe at long last got its own station, of simple but functional design, being situated at 6m 30c (from Darlington Parkgate Junction) almost at the point where the Clarence Railway joined the S&D in 1833. The up platform actually stands astride the extended Clarence formation dating from the 1870s alterations, when the formation was widened and the two routes made to run parallel to each other before actually joining together at Simpasture Junction box, the site of which was approximately at 7m 0c. Simpasture box (minus its junction to Stillington) actually lasted until 21st May 1969 because it formed the southern outlet from Shildon yard. A frequent Darlington-Bishop Auckland DMU service serves Heighington and Shildon (most trains now run to and from Saltburn) and since Shildon Works closed down the only regular freight trains left are those between Darlington and the Blue Circle cement works at Eastgate (in Weardale).

At the Bowesfield end of the line Bowesfield box is still there but it now commands a very much simplified and reduced junction layout, being a mere shadow of its former self. Even the original 1825 S&D line to the wharf at Stockton has gone; the Wharf Branch closed in 1967, and the rail connections to South Stockton goods depot were

52

Fig. 51   Cavalcade procession almost 'ready for the off' from Shildon Works, 31st August 1975 — looking towards Masons Arms. (Note ex-NER tank loco 1310 did not take part in the procession.)

(Courtesy: British Rail)

Fig. 52   North Eastern workhorse class T2 (Q6) 0-8-0 2238 (BR63395) in the Cavalcade procession 31st August 1975, passing Shildon Laden Yard Receptions site.   *(Courtesy: British Rail)*

Fig. 53   Another mainstay of North Eastern freight-class P3 (J27) 0-6-0 2392 (BR 65894) during the Cavalcade procession 31st August 1975, passing Shildon Laden Yard site.   *(Courtesy: British Rail)*

Fig 54   NER class P2 0-6-0 (J26) 406 (BR 65761) heading away from Bowesfield with a Newport-Darlington freight on 13th April 1935. Note electrification masts.   *(Courtesy: W. Rogerson)*

Fig 55   Class B1 4-6-0 61240 passing Bowesfield with a Saltburn-Darlington train c1955. Note electrification extension to rear of signal box (which still exists).   *(Courtesy: J.W. Armstrong)*

removed as recently as 1985. Now only the 1830 S&D Middlesbrough extension remains as the main line. The goods lines of 1875/76 from Stockton Cut (to Bowesfield) went on 10th July 1983 and at the same time some new main line connections, power worked by Tees Box, were installed west of Thornaby station which effectively meant that the goods lines over the additional Tees Bridge could only then give access to and from the 1863 Hartburn Curve towards Stockton. (They have since been removed completely.) However, following the rationalisation and resignalling at Eaglescliffe on 22nd March 1969, also at Stockton on 18th November 1973, the area of control exercised by Bowesfield box was considerably extended. It now controls trains on the former Leeds Northern route between Eaglescliffe and Stockton — the outpost boxes to which it works being at Picton (in the Northallerton direction), Urlay Nook (towards Darlington) and Norton South (following closure from 7th December 1986 of the box at North Shore situated where the original 1833 Stockton Branch of the Clarence was joined in 1852 by the Leeds Northern).

This then concludes just over 150 years of Shildon-Newport history which represents a saga of continual change; we have come a long way from the horse drawn chaldron wagons of the 1820s and the primitive steam locomotives which a decade later superseded the horse as a prime mover. Develop-

ment of the steam locomotive proceeded during the 19th century and well into the 20th, and then there was the short lived electrification interlude which disappeared over fifty years ago. Now the heavy freight trains of the present day are composed of high capacity continuously braked vehicles hauled by powerful diesel locomotives capable of pulling massive loads. Such is progress — this cannot be denied — yet it is not without a twinge of sadness that one contemplates the empty open spaces which were formerly Shildon's large and bustling marshalling yards, and ponders upon the vastly changed circumstances around Shildon and its closed wagon works, once the hub of the S&D system, despite efforts made recently to introduce alternative industry to the site. Likewise it is easy to mourn the passing of the Simpasture and Castle Eden Branches but the elimination of such duplicate routes was the inevitable result of the radically altered circumstances which faced the railways during the 1960s.

However on a slightly more optimistic note, it is still possible to see the Eastgate cement trains passing the site of Simpasture Junction near Newton Aycliffe and to observe (for how much longer?) the occasional freights rumbling through Stillington where a century ago the traffic volume was so heavy as to justify quadruple tracking. Happily Bowesfield Junction remains as the focal point for Tees-side, still with plenty of trains moving around, but Tees Yard as it is now, compared with how it was in all its

Fig 56   Another pre-colour light signalling view at Bowesfield c1954 with class A5 4-6-2T 69831 passing on a Darlington-Saltburn train.
(Courtesy: A.R. Thompson)

glory when newly opened in 1963, presents rather a sorry sight. The Up Yard control tower has disappeared altogether and so have the up reception lines; the Down Yard too is a shadow of its former self, hump shunting has ceased and the reception lines have vanished. At the present time a still significant volume of Speedlink traffic is dealt with in a reduced group of the former Up Yard sorting sidings, and some room is left for staging purposes — also sidings for use by BR's own engineering departments.

The railway's freight business of the 1970s and 80s is a totally different ball game from what it was during the two previous decades; the emphasis is now very much focussed upon bulk movement in block train loads, complemented by the Freightliner and Speedlink network, thus the 1960s style large marshalling yards no longer earn their keep and really do not have a place in the latter day 20th century railway scene. Tees-side itself, once a thriving area of industrial growth, seems to be in the economic doldrums, and Middlesbrough — the success story of the 19th century — currently suffers

from an above national average unemployment problem. The prosperity of the North East's railways and the future prospects of the territory which they serve are inextricably linked, so one must earnestly hope that a significant upturn in Tees-side's industrial fortunes occurs before too long — before even more of the local freight railway network vanishes into oblivion.

It must be said, however, that BR's Railfreight Sector has achieved success in maximising both its market penetration and use of resources around Tees-side, albeit with a relatively small dedicated fleet of Thornaby based diesel locomotives and greatly reduced levels of manpower, infrastructure and rolling stock than was previously the case. In fact, Railfreight has risen like a phoenix from the ashes of the former wagon load business, and the positive attitudes currently being displayed towards the freight side of railway affairs surely must augur well for the future. One sincerely hopes so!

6. THE ROUTES DESCRIBED

6.1 Shildon to Newport

The electrified route commenced within the Shildon Works complex where No 3 Roundhouse (which dated from 1891/92) was specially adapted and wired up in 1915 to house the ten strong electric locomotive fleet. Each stall had a number above it to indicate where individual locomotives should stand, though apparently in practice they clustered around the turntable in any order! Following closure of Shildon motive power depot in 1935, the premises were incorporated into the Wagon Works (and by 1938 had been converted to other uses) and for this reason the former engine sheds cannot now be readily distinguished from the rest of the works buildings.

Shildon Works emerged from small beginnings being located not far from the place where the S&D used to change over between stationary winding engine and locomotive haulage at the foot of Brusselton incline; though the story of its subsequent development, and how Shildon's most famous personage — Timothy Hackworth — influenced events, is really beyond the scope of this book. Suffice it to say that by 1897 the NER decided to concentrate much of its wagon building work here and thereafter Shildon Works grew in importance (the relatively recent building of MGR wagons in large numbers demonstrates this point) until it fell victim to the prevailing 1980's style of business economics which resulted in closure during June 1984 — with the loss of some 2500 jobs. The site is now designated 'Hackworth Industrial Park' — a wall plaque proudly proclaims its formal opening on 28th October 1985 by David Mitchell MP, Parliamentary Under Secretary of State for Transport — but so far it has hardly come up to expectations despite strenuous efforts made by the local authority (Sedgefield District Council).

Just outside the Works area, the rail tracks crossed Redworth Road at what became known as Masons Arms level crossing. Hereabouts the S&D's inaugural train started its epic journey to Stockton on Tuesday 27th September 1825, and from roughly the same place British Rail's brilliantly staged Rail 150 Cavalcade procession bound for Heighington duly set off on Sunday 31st August 1975. Masons Arms public house, situated on the corner of Strand Street immediately adjacent to the level crossing, became part of the S&D passenger station in 1833 until the present Shildon station on the Bishop Auckland line opened in 1842. However, the name 'Mason's Arms' has recently been changed to 'New Masons', and although the tracks on either side of the crossing have now been removed, the exit from the works site is still guarded by a rather lonely but quite modern looking semaphore signal!

Continuing along from Masons Arms past the former goods yard, the ruins of the S&D coal drops can still be seen near the fork of the junction with the Bishop Auckland line. These were used for coaling locomotives right up to the closure of Shildon shed in 1935. The Bishop Auckland line (one of the S&D's numerous extensions) joined the original S&D route at a junction (recently lifted) situated near to Spout Lane overbridge where on the up side (the line direction is 'up' from Bishop Auckland to Darlington) stands Shildon's only signal box — in fact the only signal box left in this area for it now controls what is left at Bishop Auckland station (just one short platform!) and the remaining portion of the Weardale Branch which is still used by cement trains to and from Eastgate.

Beyond Spout Lane bridge the formation widened considerably into the marshalling yard site, the larger Laden Yard being on the up (north) side of the passenger lines and the rather smaller Empties Yard — together with its continuation along to West Sidings parallel with the Wagon Works Branch — on the down (south) side. Part of the Laden Yard site formed the original Thickley Weigh siding where traffic was first exchanged between the S&D and Clarence Railways, and following an initial enlargement of the sidings during the 1850s, the marshalling yards as such were laid down a decade later and brought into use in 1869. The passenger lines were diverted to run through the middle of the site — hence the reverse curves still evident today — and the centre of the yards was marked by an extremely lengthy footbridge (Hildyards Bridge) which still stands and shows all the signs of having been extended more than once. The original cast iron bridge portion bears the legend "HARRIS MDCCCLVII MAKER" (ie 1857) and thus predates the major alterations of 1869 by twelve years. Beyond Hildyards Bridge were the Laden Yard sorting and departure sidings which terminated just before

Fig 57   Shildon Yards. 19th century view looking west. Laden Yard Receptions to right and Empties Yard left.
(Courtesy: Durham County Record Office)

Fig 58   Shildon Yards. 19th century view looking east. Laden Yard Sorting Sidings to left and Empties Yard
right.   *(Courtesy: Durham County Record Office)*

reaching an overbridge carrying a minor road — now little better than a rough track — reached via Walker Lane from Middridge village. This bridge (which still carries some traces of electrification ironwork) was the background scene to some vintage electric train photographs — a couple of which are included in this book — and the yard outlet continued independently from the passenger lines until Simpasture Junction was reached half a mile further along. Until the yards closed in 1935 arrivals for the Empties Yard could be turned in off the down passenger line at a box known as Middridge, but subsequently any Shildon bound freights had to run inside at Shildon box and back into the Empties Yard. The tracks in the Laden Yard were all removed by the mid 1970s and the site formed an ideal viewing area complete with a temporary grandstand erected for the 1975 Cavalcade procession, while the Empties Yard and West Sidings remained in use until 1984 for the reception, grading, and shunting of wagons for Shildon Works. Track lifting was not finally completed until 1986.

No traces now remain of Simpasture Junction, apart from a few ominous looking fissures in the ground on the up (north) side of the formation which mark the mid-1950s underground fire. Actually the box here survived the 1963 closure of the branch towards Stillington lasting until 21st May 1969 because it controlled the outlet from Shildon Yard for movements proceeding towards Darlington. A disused high loading dock for the former 'Old Town Quarry' can still be seen on the down (south) side of the line; the box stood on the opposite side slightly east thereof. The junction site was established around 1875/6 following the acquisition of additional land to enable widening of the original formation, thus the Simpasture Branch thereafter ran parallel with the S&D for about half a mile (49 chains) before turning left into a shallow cutting behind what is now the up platform at Newton Aycliffe halt (opened 9th January 1978). From this parting of the ways between the S&D and the Clarence tracks the S&D curves sharply away to the right, and the bridge just around the corner with modern looking metal girders placed above stone abutments marks the spot where a serious collision occurred in the early hours of 16th November 1949. The 5.10am Crook-Darlington passenger train ran into the rear portion of a divided freight train on the up line at 5.43am; the resultant collision demolished the stone arch of Bridge No 9, situated 1340 yards from Simpasture box.

From Simpasture Junction through to Newport the line direction was 'down' (so is the line direction from Ferryhill to Norton West) and the gradient fell away towards Stillington Junction at an average of

1 in 200 for the first two miles followed by 1 in 451 for another three miles or so. It is possible to walk along the abandoned track-bed, now a well defined footpath, from just beyond Newton Aycliffe halt (where one parapet of a Clarence Railway over-bridge, now filled in and grassed over, can be seen) to the A167 (old A1) road bridge near Travellers Rest. The formation actually runs between the former munitions factory site — now a light industrial estate — and Newton Aycliffe 'new' town, but no traces exist at all of the former wartime station at Simpasture (East), its junction and layout, nor its signal box which stood on the up (south) side in the 'vee' between the running lines and the passenger station spur. It is also interesting to speculate that the projected Deanery Branch — had it been built — would have left the Clarence 'main' line somewhere in this locality.

A little further on it is still possible to see the site of School Aycliffe level crossing, and the stopped up roadways on either side of the line, then the next feature of note is where the formation is carried over St Cuthbert's Way by a still imposing bridge of metal construction opened on October 10th 1956. Shortly afterwards, just prior to reaching the now bricked up overbridge carrying the A167 (old A1) road it is still possible to discern the junction site at Demons Bridge, though all traces of the wartime station have gone. A solitary brick building on the up (south) side — once the lamproom which stood alongside Demons Bridge box — is all that is left. Immediately to the east of this overbridge is the site of Travellers Rest level crossing where the old A1 road used to cross the railway, and this area together with the former roadway approaches is now occupied by Durham County Highways Dept and called 'Aycliffe Store'. The box here stood derelict for many years on the up (south) side of the line, becoming disused in 1942 after the new A1 road bridge was completed. Actually procedural formalities for stopping up the roadway which passed over the line were not completed until 1944, and for the immediate road approaches thereto not until 1956!

For another half mile from Travellers Rest the formation is in private ownership, until Ricknall Mill crossing site is reached where Ricknall Lane — a minor road leading to Great Stainton — passed across the line. Soon afterwards the formation runs on an embankment and it crossed over the East Coast Main Line by a substantial girder bridge (which was renewed prior to the 1915 electrification) of which only the stone abutments now stand. Immediately beyond the ECML overbridge was the site of Aycliffe sub-station where on the up (south) side of the Simpasture Branch the derelict ruins stood until the late 1960s. Absolutely no traces of the sub-station now remain though it is possible to identify the plot of land where it once stood immediately adjacent to what is now the 'Blacksmith's Arms' public house. (The NER sought powers to purchase the additional land here in 1914.)

A short way past the sub-station site the formation is broken and a minor road leading to Preston le Skerne is carried over the A1(M) dual carriageway by a bridge constructed almost in a direct line with the former railway embankment. Thereafter the site of Preston Lane level crossing can still be discerned adjacent to a relatively new electric sub-station belonging to the NEEB and called 'Skerneside'. The small gate box (which later became a block post between 1941 and 1951) once controlled a siding here connected with the down (eastbound) line where constructional materials for the electrification scheme were unloaded. For the next couple of miles or so the formation is mostly in private ownership also generally inaccessible, and it is broken again immediately prior to reaching the erstwhile Elstob Lane level crossing where a highway improvement scheme now takes the Great Stainton-Sedgefield road over the site of the disused line. There was once a public siding here on the up (south) side where agricultural traffic could be loaded until the late 1920s. The former gate house at Elstob is now an imposing private residence, and from here to the next crossing over Bishopton Lane the route is privately owned (suitably accompanied by warning notices against unauthorised entry!).

Picking up the route again at Bishopton Lane where the Bishopton-Sedgefield road crossed the line on the level, a row of ex-railway houses can be seen on the down (north) side. A small brick built crossing hut with outside lever frame used to stand on the up (south) side, and less than a quarter of a mile further on the present line from Ferryhill to Norton West (the Clarence Railway's 1834 City of Durham branch) joins the Simpasture Branch formation at Stillington Junction — Stillington North from 1928. The signal box stood in the 'vee' between the two routes and it was from here to Carlton West Junction that the track was quadrupled in 1885. The newer Mineral Lines were on the south side of the formation and on the north side there was once a long through siding (later called the Down Independent) which connected with the Down Main Line by means of a ground frame outlet — latterly released by Stillington North box — situated near to the site of the original station known as 'Stillington Weigh'. Now nothing remains apart from the Ferryhill-Norton West double track which continues towards Stillington station, before which the original structure of a Clarence Railway bridge over a farm road can be seen on the down (north) side of the line

(the corresponding bridgework on the up (south) side dates from the 1880s widening). The down side bridge parapet bears a faded and worn inscription "Davison Bridge 1831" — so named after the late John Robert Davison, a prominent landowner in this locality around the time the Clarence Railway was originally constructed.

The latter day Stillington station was of the island platform type, constructed in 1884 in conjunction with the track widening scheme. It replaced a traditional type of two platform country station on roughly the same site. Originally called 'Carlton Ironworks' station it was renamed 'Stillington' on 1st November 1879 and lost its regular passenger trains when the Stockton-Ferryhill-Spennymoor service ceased from 31st March 1952. Public closure for goods traffic took place from 5th July 1965 though wagon load traffic for the adjacent private sidings continued to be dealt with well into the 1970s. The Carlton Ironworks were originally established here in 1866 but in 1920 the Carlton Iron Company passed into the hands of Messrs Dorman Long, soon to become Tees-side's major iron and steel company. Unfortunately by 1929 this take-over resulted in closure, Carlton Ironworks being one of the numerous casualties of the pre-war depression years. Subsequently the site was put to other uses, first by a firm known as Stillite Products and later by Darchem Industries. The present occupants no longer use rail transport and the small network of private sidings, along with the goods yard have since been abandoned.

From 18th October 1964 the additional mineral lines were put out of use and a portion removed a short distance east of Stillington in conjunction with road bridge reconstruction; following completion of signalling alterations at Stillington they were officially dispensed with from 1st August 1965. Shortly afterwards the passenger station was demolished and a significant realignment of track took place with the result that the present day up and down lines actually run in the mineral lines formation hereabouts. The signal box located on the down side is still operative though normally switched out and only opened specially to shorten the long block section between Ferryhill and Norton West during periods when ECML trains are diverted this way.

The gradient falls from approaching Stillington Junction to Carlton at a continuous 1 in 230 for some four miles, and the next station at Carlton (Redmarshall from 1st July 1923) was of the island platform type, like Stillington, also constructed under the track widening scheme of the mid-1880s. Originally Carlton Lane in early Clarence Railway days, this was once a two platform station and until

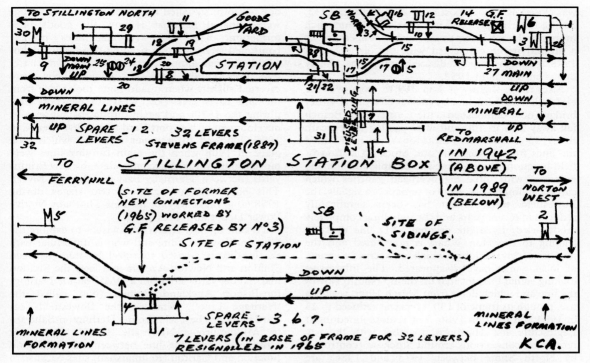

Drawing 11   Signalling sketches to show the effects of track rationalisation. Stillington Station signal box in 1942 and 1989.
(Courtesy: Author's Collection)

the track widening there was a level crossing here. Redmarshall was closed to passengers from 31st March 1952 upon withdrawal of the Stockton-Ferryhill-Spennymoor service but remained open for freight until 15th September 1958. Demolition of the island platform commenced on 6th November 1966 and following the closure of the box on 25th November 1967, together with subsequent removal of the mineral lines and associated double junctions, a major track realignment took place thus all traces of the former station have completely disappeared.

Shortly afterwards, at the site of Carlton West Junction, the abandoned Newport formation of 1877 turns away from the existing route towards Norton West and climbing slightly at 1 in 289 is soon joined by the derelict 1878 Castle Eden branch (from Wellfield) at Redmarshall South. Again no traces remain of the junction, or the signal box which stood on the down (east) side, though the site can still be viewed from the adjacent road bridge (Letch Lane) — even though the scenery has been altered somewhat by an overhead pipeline and additional electricity pylons constructed since closure of the railway in 1968. From this point the long descent commenced towards Bowesfield, firstly at 1 in 103

for nearly a couple of miles then easing to 1 in 472 thereafter. Under the permissive block regulations which were applicable on this branch, the crews of both steam and electric loose coupled heavy mineral trains had quite a job on their hands to maintain control down this stretch, particularly when they could see a train in front (or its tail lamps during darkness).

The course of the line runs through post-war housing development north west of Stockton and part of it now forms a designated cycle and pedestrian route — the 'Stockton Cycleway' — as between the (now demolished) road bridges at Harrowgate Lane and Fairfield (Oxbridge Lane). Approaching Hartburn the substantial brick built bridge which once carried the formation over the Stockton-Darlington main road has disappeared, and immediately afterwards is the site of Bowesfield West Junction where the short-lived Hartburn West curve of 1901-03 struck off to join the former Leeds Northern route of 1852 at Hartburn West Junction. The line of boundary fencing still marks the outline of this curve, part of which until the early 1930s remained as a brickyard siding. Bowesfield West box, which stood on the down (east) side of the line, was closed as a block post from 24th October 1932, having latterly only been open for a few hours each morning, though it remained capable of operation as a ground frame connected with the up line until 1948 (though largely disused) and was finally demolished around 1952.

After rising slightly at 1 in 319 to cross over the ex-Leeds Northern line by means of a metal girder bridge (now demolished), the Castle Eden Branch fell away at 1 in 150 and after passing underneath the A135 (former A19) Stockton-Yarm road joined the lines from Eaglescliffe and Stockton at Bowesfield Junction. Once a large and complicated looking junction, with three big overhead gantries which carried an impressive array of semaphore signals, the Bowesfield track layout has been significantly reduced in recent years and the signalling completely modernised. Even the original S&D line of 1825 leading to Stockton Wharf is now lifted and the numerous private sidings which once served a variety of local works have disappeared. The impressive looking signal box, located on the up (south) side of the line and which dates from March 1905, is still in use, though its frame of 130 levers was reduced to 45 in 1984 and to 36 in 1986. The remote junctions at Eaglescliffe and Hartburn, together with the few remaining connections around Stockton (controlled by North Shore between 1973 and 1986) are operated by means of miniature 'individual function switches' (IFS). The manual frame was removed altogether during April 1989 after a further simplification was completed; nevertheless, Bowesfield is still a busy and important box.

East of Bowesfield the S&D Middlesbrough extension of 1830 — quadruple track until 1988 — soon crosses the Tees by two separate bridges, the southernmost of these being the 1906/7 replacement using the piers of the 1844 bridge (which superseded the original 1830 suspension bridge) and is still in use. The northernmost structure (now out of use) was a product of the 1882 track widening and road improvements scheme between Tees Bridge and South Stockton (Thornaby from 1892), which also included construction of a large new island platform station and replacement of two level crossings by road bridges.

Thornaby station, a huge island platform, is now unstaffed and bereft of buildings apart from the modern shelters one usually associates with unstaffed halts. A large manual signal box called Thornaby East stood at the Middlesbrough end of the station between 1908 and 1963. From hereon the formation widens out into the Tees Yard complex and Thornaby motive power depot. Originally the two running lines and the pre-1882 South Stockton passenger station (which only had one platform signalled for either direction working) were situated in what is now the goods lines formation. The main running lines initially continued straight along heading due eastwards for Middlesbrough almost in the alignment of the latter day Tees Down Yard Receptions. They were diverted slightly when quadrupling took place from the Old River (Newport West) to Newport East during the 1870s and again during the subsequent development of Newport Yard which first opened in 1875, followed by a major diversion which took place in 1908 when the main running lines were moved southwards to accommodate the new Erimus yards (between Thornaby East and the Old River). This happened yet again in two stages during 1958/60 to make way for the new Thornaby Motive Power Depot and Tees Yards.

To sum up: any reader who wishes to explore the Shildon-Newport route and who is unfamiliar with the locality is advised to travel by train between Shildon and Newton Aycliffe and view the Shildon marshalling yards site from a DMU on the Darlington-Bishop Auckland Branch (now called the 'Heritage Line'). Similarly the Bowesfield-Tees Yard section is best seen from a Darlington-Saltburn or Middlesbrough-Newcastle DMU. It is not possible to walk the line between the Stillington Junction and Carlton (Redmarshall) sites because to do so would involve trespass alongside an operative railway; nevertheless both the Stillington and Redmarshall station sites can be viewed from adjacent public roads, and Whitton bridge on the Stillington-Redmarshall road is a good vantage point for a general overview of the former 'widened' section. Anyone wishing to travel over the Stockton-Ferryhill route can only do so by means of ECML diverted trains (between York and Newcastle) usually on selected Sunday mornings, provided dates and times are chosen with great care!

It is still possible to explore the abandoned Simpasture Branch between Newton Aycliffe halt and the A167 (old A1) road near the site of Travellers Rest crossing where a reasonable walkway exists, but from thereon much of the formation towards Stillington is either in private ownership and/or impassable, though the adjacent surroundings at the former Ricknall Mill, Preston Lane, Elstob and Bishopton Lane crossings can be viewed from public roads. Finally it is still possible to walk from the site of Redmarshall South almost to Bowesfield West near Hartburn, and the concluding stretch towards Bowesfield can be seen quite well from the A135 (old A19) overbridge on the Stockton-Yarm road. Ordnance Survey map sheet 93 'Middlesbrough and Darlington' adequately covers the course of all lines described in this book.

6.2 Wellfield to Redmarshall

An empty space between the original Durham-Hartlepool road and the new A181 Wellfield by-pass which has been built over the abandoned railway formation, marks the spot where Wellfield station once stood. The junction site can still be seen immediately south of the bridge underneath the original Durham road, and until Wellfield station was opened in 1882 the signal box here was called Castle Eden North Junction. The first signal box stood on top of the embankment on the up (east) side of the line opposite to the junction points but in 1910 a new and enlarged box was built situated at the north end of the up platform.

The first railway at Wellfield actually dated from 1835; it came from Hartlepool via Castle Eden and was joined in 1878 by the Castle Eden Branch from Carlton and Bowesfield via Wynyard. Last traces of the branch disappeared in 1969 following closure of

the remaining portion to Wingate South, where after 1966 a reversal was involved to gain access to Trimdon Grange Colliery, though the 'main' line in the Hartlepool direction lasted for another ten years until it finally succumbed on 31st December 1979. The passenger service between Wellfield and Stockton, inaugurated on 1st March 1880, ceased from 2nd November 1931, though Wellfield station continued to be served by Sunderland-West Hartlepool trains until 9th June 1952. The line direction from Wellfield to the junctions at Redmarshall was 'up'.

Leaving the abandoned Wellfield Junction site the line climbed at 1 in 270 for almost two miles towards Wingate South. Part of the formation can still be followed for about half a mile, then it disappears and cannot be traced again until well after the site of Wingate South Junction. In fact one cannot now see

Fig 59   NER class S3 4-6-0 (B16/1) 2372 (BR 61443) running round an enthusiasts special at Wellfield September 1956.

(Courtesy: J.W. Armstrong)

63

Fig 60   NER class T2 0-8-0 (Q6) 2230 (BR 63387) in action approaching Wellfield with a train of empties from Hartlepool for Hawthorne (South Hetton) in August 1967. (The branch from Redmarshall direction trailed in from the right.)

(Courtesy: P.J. Robinson)

exactly where this route crossed over the top of the older Hartlepool-Ferryhill line, and it is extremely difficult to locate the site of Wingate South, either the junction or the box, the formation having undergone radical change due to housing developments.

However, a short distance south of Wingate South (the village hereabouts is actually called Station Town!) it is possible to pick up the formation again near the summit of the line. From hereon the line falls all the way to Thorpe Thewles viaduct — some 8 miles further on — at varying gradients mostly around 1 in 100/110/132/165/173.

Of the three intermediate stations on the branch, Hurworth Burn still has both platforms but no buildings, Wynyard has buildings on the down side but no platforms, and Thorpe Thewles has only the up platform and the former Station Master's house. Each station had the usual country goods yard and coal depot facilities and remained open for freight business until 2nd April 1951, almost twenty years after closure for passengers. Much of the formation

between Hurworth Burn and Wynyard can still be followed, but it is physically broken just north of Wynyard station due to improvements in the A689 Sedgefield-Hartlepool road. Wynyard station itself is privately owned and for about half a mile towards Thorpe Thewles the former railway route is inaccessible. It is now necessary to make a detour here through Tilery Wood which forms the northern end of the 'Castle Eden Walkway'.

The 'Castle Eden Walkway' was inspired by Cleveland County Council who acquired the abandoned track-bed in 1977 and have since transformed it into an extremely pleasant nature trail. From about half a mile south of Wynyard station it is possible to follow the line's course for about three miles to Thorpe Thewles station and the site of the viaduct, the walkway having proved to be a very popular and well used social amenity. At Thorpe Thewles (where only the up platform now remains) adequate car parking facilities have been created together with a picnic area. The station house is now used as a community nature trail centre, and a

Fig 61   Thorpe Thewles station shortly before closure of the line as a through route in 1966. The station buildings have since been restored to their former glory and they form the focal point of the Castle Eden Walkway and Nature Trail.   *(Courtesy: Durham County Record Office)*

project to reconstruct the former office and waiting room has restored the station building to something nearly like its original appearance. A reasonable footpath exists between Thorpe Thewles station and the viaduct site; also another footpath climbs out of the 'viaduct bottoms' to regain the abandoned formation near the former Redmarshall North Junction.

The line crossed the Thorpe Beck valley by means of an imposing brick viaduct of twenty arches constructed during the late 1870s. There was also a smaller viaduct of three arches nearby, and some thirteen years following closure of the railway in 1966 it was decided that these structures should be blown up. The three arches were destroyed first on 1st April 1979 and the Thorpe Thewles by-pass on the A177 Durham-Stockton road now passes through this break in the formation. The main viaduct did not come down so easily; after the first attempt made to blow it up on 3rd June 1979 much of the structure remained stubbornly in position, and it required another explosion on 10th June 1979 to finish it off so the area could be cleared.

One can still view the junction site at Redmarshall North — the box was on the down (west) side — and in a deep cutting at the junction with the operational Ferryhill-Norton railway close to where Redmarshall East box once stood, a rusty derelict junction bracket signal post (of no great antiquity!) was still in evidence quite recently. The gradient rose slightly at 1 in 300 from Thorpe Thewles viaduct towards Redmarshall South, but it fell away sharply at 1 in 100 between Redmarshall North and East junctions. Both on the Redmarshall North-East curve, also between Redmarshall North and South, the formation's appearance has been drastically changed since closure by the erection of additional electric pylons. Also the former metal girder bridge has been demolished which used to carry the 1878 Castle Eden Branch over the top of the much older — and still operative — Clarence Railway dating from 1833.

A visit to the Castle Eden Walkway at Thorpe Thewles (preferably in summer!) is certainly recommended to anyone wishing to recapture something of this little-known branch line's atmosphere.

Fig 62   NER class T2 0-8-0 (Q6) 2262 (BR 63419) crosses Thorpe Thewles viaduct on 11th September 1964 with the 2.33pm Mineral from Hawthorne (South Hetton) to ICI Billingham.   *(Courtesy: J.M. Boyes)*

Fig 63   Redmarshall North signal box Sunday, 12th April 1953 with 'Jubilee' class 4-6-0 45645 *Collingwood* hauling a diverted Manchester-Newcastle excursion train travelling via Wellfield due to major engineering work around West Hartlepool.   *(Courtesy: J.W. Armstrong)*

Fig 64   Redmarshall South signal box with former electrified route to left of picture and Wellfield Branch straight ahead c1954. The class K1 2-6-0 62044 is hauling a diverted Sunday express and the unidentified Pacific at rear is coasting without steam applied, the train having travelled from the Billingham direction via Norton West to Redmarshall Station (reverse) thence to Bowesfield (reverse) due to major engineering work around North Shore (Stockton).   *(Courtesy: J.W. Armstrong)*

7. FURTHER ELECTRIFICATION

7.1 The NER and Main Line Electrification

The Shildon-Newport story really needs to be considered against the wider background of the North Eastern's whole approach to electrification and the influence exerted by two of its most eminent General Managers. Thanks to the boundless energy displayed by George Stegmann Gibb, who became General Manager in 1891, the North Eastern prospered as he radically overhauled its organisation and modernised its business style. Under Gibb's leadership the North Tyneside suburban electrification came to fruition in 1904, and as the scheme justified itself over the next few years thoughts naturally turned towards possible future extensions of electric working. However, after Sir George Gibb's departure for the London Underground system in 1906 (he was knighted in 1904), one could be tempted to ask if some of the reforming zeal which characterised North Eastern affairs, particularly around the turn of the century, had been replaced by a more cautious outlook?

Under the next General Manager, Alexander Kaye Butterworth, the North Eastern continued to flourish. Indeed, right up to the outbreak of World War I in 1914, Butterworth worked long and hard — usually with success — to consolidate its strong position. Yet Gibb's former bold approach towards the electrification philosophy, so ably expounded by Charles Merz and enthusiastically supported by Vincent Raven, seemed to be no longer in evidence. Despite the apparent advantages of electrification, Butterworth displayed a degree of caution towards what he considered could amount to a high risk investment strategy. Thus a report submitted in 1908 by Messrs Merz & McLellan (who were retained by the NER as Consulting Engineers), in which electrification of the South Tyneside suburban network to Sunderland and South Shields was strongly recommended, did not gain Butterworth's support — despite the fact that a recovery of patronage lost to street tramways had become evident since the North Tyneside services were electrified.

However, in 1911 Butterworth called upon Merz & McLellan to prepare a report covering the possibility of further electrification on the NER, which led to Charles Merz and Vincent Raven visiting North America, and upon their return a comprehensive submission laid the foundations of a far reaching main line electrification concept. They extolled the advantages of electric traction over steam and suggested a major scheme involving electric locomotives. An estimated total expenditure of around £1½ million was projected. This report was put to the Board of Directors on 12th January 1912 and Butterworth followed it up with a memorandum dated 8th August 1912 in which he counselled caution and expressed the opinion that "--- the issues involved are so important and the problems to be faced so varied, while at the same time the information obtainable as to some of the results to be looked for from the change is so far from complete, that if the matter is to be proceeded with the right course is to limit the initial electrification to a short section and treat it as experimental in character". (In the event this is precisely what happened; Shildon-Newport was a self-contained system which readily lent itself to being treated as an 'experiment'.)

Butterworth was even quoted as having expressed a viewpoint to the effect that he wondered whether there was any case for having an experiment at all "--- in view of all the experience gained by other Companies and the body of knowledge developed by electrical engineers". Another source credited him with saying that Shildon-Newport was suggested because if the scheme failed not a great deal of damage would have been done nor money wasted! It is interesting to note in this regard that both Gibb and Butterworth originally were lawyers by profession, but unlike Gibb, Butterworth was perhaps more of a lawyer than a railwayman. While he did not stamp his imprint upon railway affairs and display as high a profile as Gibb, Butterworth's utterly dedicated no-nonsense approach ensured sound business growth, thus pre-World War I the NER was among the most powerful and influential in the pre-grouping railway league table (and in 1914 he too received a knighthood).

During the first decade of this century the Midland, L&Y, and LBSC, together with the London Underground had all jumped aboard the suburban electrification band-wagon, but the NER definitely pointed the way forward with its Shildon-Newport scheme, a pioneering installation impressive by any standards, destined to be the forerunner of greater things to come.

In 1919, following Sir Vincent Raven's return from secondment to government service during World War I, Merz & McLellan came up with yet another memorandum which dealt with further extended electric working on the NER. This time they had empirical data (ie practical experience as opposed to theory) derived from Shildon-Newport to work on, so in joint authorship with Henry Angus Watson (General Superintendent) Raven produced a lengthy report (dated October 1919) entitled "Report on Proposed Electrification of Main Line York-Newcastle with intermediary feeders". They opened with a general summary in which was outlined the case for the scheme, and the experience gained from the Shildon-Newport operation was recounted. Justification was demonstrated to support Raven's contention that 5 electrics could do the work of 13 steam locomotives in given comparative circumstances as between October 1913 and October 1918. The report went on to say that the Shildon-Newport results encouraged consideration of electrification over the York-Newcastle main line plus the associated loop between Northallerton, Eaglescliffe, Stockton and Ferryhill totalling some 110 route miles. Messrs Raven and Watson went on to explain that main line traffic was so dense, and the locomotive workings to a large extent self contained, that the majority of trains would work through (between York and Newcastle) without the necessity of changing intermediately from electric to steam haulage as would be the case if only a short section was electrified (eg York-Darlington).

In a section of the report headed 'Line Equipment' the authors set out comparative costs between third rail and overhead wiring. For example, it was stated that third rail would cost £2850 per track mile compared against £4340 per track mile for overhead wires. Maintenance costs were, however, stated to be higher for third rail than for overhead viz: £93 compared against £74 per track mile. They recommended that third rail be used, with certain of the larger stations and yards being overhead viz: York Station, York Yards, Thirsk, Northallerton, Darlington, Ferryhill, Durham, Low Fell, Newcastle Central and Stockton, and estimated that some 282 track miles would be third rail with 115 track miles of overhead wire conduction. Shunting locomotives would work either on batteries or overhead wire conductors as appropriate.

A typical day's freight working (27th March 1919) was re-cast and the exercise revealed that 142 freight trains could have been worked electrically. A passenger working comparison was based on the last normal timetable ie May 1914, as train services applicable in 1919 could not be taken as typical due to immediate post-war conditions. This simulation exercise demonstrated that 29 electrics would do the work of 54 steam on passenger trains and on the selected day 80 electric freight locomotives would have sufficed against 155 steam. A total of 109 electrics against 209 steam looked most impressive, but in the financial equations which followed it emerged that a huge initial outlay was involved — something of the order of £1 million plus for line equipment alone — before one even considered maintenance charges and the capital cost to provide a fleet of electric locomotives at around £12-13000 apiece (off-set of course by savings in steam locomotive building). On the other side of the coin, the joint authors conveyed a veiled warning that much of the York-Newcastle main line would need to be quadrupled if electrification was not progressed, and towards the end of 1919 provisional approval was forthcoming from the Board of Directors.

It is also interesting to note a subsequent change in policy from third rail to overhead: Raven apparently found that leakage problems could give rise to concern in that current (especially at high voltages) has a tendency to leak to earth if near the ground and it was feared that wastage could be unacceptably high with a 1500v DC third rail main line. Thus in spite of first cost advantages, overhead wires were now seen as preferable to third rail and the scheme was amended accordingly.

So once again Raven set sail across the Atlantic (this time accompanied by Mr F. Lydall of M&M), his mission being to inspect the current North American electric locomotive building and running techniques, but before he went he sought authority to construct a prototype electric main line passenger locomotive. Upon receipt of approval on 18th March 1920 design work was immediately put in hand. The machine was duly ordered on 26th January 1921 and it first saw the light of day in May 1922 — No 13 had arrived! Following Messrs Raven and Lydall's return, they reported in October 1920 upon the various types of electric locomotive seen during their travels; it was mainly a technical report containing facts rather than specific recommendations.

By late 1920 the outlook for the North Eastern's main line scheme had become decidedly bleak. Apart from the unsettled post-World War I economic situation which inhibited capital investment of the scale necessary to get a project of this magnitude off the ground, external influences were at work in the shape of the newly created Ministry of Transport — which was formed in September 1919 and overtook the railway functions previously dealt with by the

Board of Trade. The first Minister of Transport, Eric Campbell Geddes (another ex-North Eastern officer!) decided to appoint a Committee with a remit not only to enquire generally into railway electrification, but also to specify standards for future development. Meanwhile, the North Eastern was asked to shelve their main line electrification plans pending the outcome of the Committee's report. This Committee was chaired by Sir Alexander Kennedy (Charles Merz was one of its members!); it first met on 22nd March 1920 and its interim report dated 12th July was published on 29th September. The original terms of reference were further extended in October 1920, and in its final report dated 30th June 1921 the 'Kennedy Committee' pronounced that the standard for new main line electrification should henceforth be 1500v DC allowing for continuance of existing schemes which were different (such as the LBSC suburban lines).

The Kennedy report was mainly technical in nature but in point of fact it recommended the very things which Merz and McLellan had already proposed to the NER! The timing and results of this Committee were, upon reflection, cruelly ironic to Sir Vincent Raven. By the time No 13 emerged from Darlington North Road Works in May 1922 his whole York-Newcastle scheme was overshadowed by numerous adverse factors, not least of which was the Railways Act of 1921 which heralded the North Eastern's demise as a separate railway company.

Undaunted, Sir Vincent Raven spared no effort in getting the electrification message across. Probably his first public pronouncement appeared in the February 1919 *Proceedings of the Institution of Electrical Engineers,* but he really went to town with a thorough-going exposition delivered to the North East Coast Institution of Engineers and Shipbuilders at Newcastle on 16th December 1921. This memorable paper, and the subsequent discussion it provoked, was widely and favourably reported upon in the contemporary railway technical press, and he followed this up with a comprehensive paper (delivered on 14th June 1922) at the 1922 summer meeting of the Institution of Mechanical Engineers held in Paris. Raven even presented a paper to the GWR Debating Society on 4th January 1923, after having given a similar presentation on home ground to the NER Lecture and Debating Society at York on 25th January 1921.

Despite Raven's pioneering spirit, and all his praiseworthy efforts in the cause of electrification, attempts to launch a million pounds plus venture in the prevailing financial and economic scenario stood no chance. By the time the grouping came along in January 1923 the scheme was as good as dead. (It is interesting to reflect that had this scheme been implemented it most probably would have included an extension from Eaglescliffe to Bowesfield to interface with Shildon-Newport and so permit access to/from Newport Yards. Also presumably all four tracks of the quadrupled section between Carlton (Redmarshall) and Stillington Junction (later Stillington North) might well have been electrified?)

7.2 Towards the ultimate choice — DC or AC

By 1927 the Ministry of Transport had set up another committee of enquiry (The Railway Electrification Committee), chaired by Colonel Sir J.W. Pringle, the then Chief Inspecting Officer of Railways. Its terms of reference were to review the recommendations of the earlier Kennedy Committee and they were "--- enjoined to pay regard to what modifications, if any, should be made having regard to developments which have since taken place." The 'Pringle Committee' in its findings published in 1928 said much the same thing as the previous one some seven years earlier. (It is perhaps worthy of note that Charles Merz also sat on this committee, and another famous member was Mr H.N. (later Sir Nigel) Gresley.)

Within a relatively short space of time yet another committee of enquiry was appointed, chaired by Lord Weir of Eastwood and given a much wider remit. The Weir Committee — of which Sir Ralph Wedgewood was a member (Wedgewood succeeded Butterworth as General Manager of the NER in 1922 and at the grouping became Chief General Manager of the LNER) — noted in their report dated 24th March 1931 "--- with the exception of a small section of mineral line on the LNER some 18 route miles in length [ie Shildon-Newport] no main line electrification has taken place in Great Britain". They accepted the 1928 Pringle Committee recommendation about 1500v DC (overhead) henceforth being the standard, and concluded that electric traction is superior to steam (in complete vindication of what Raven had been saying some 10 years earlier). The report went on to cite all the advantages of main line electrification but made no specific recommendations apart from expressing the general view (echoed by a future British Railways Board (BRB) Chairman — Sir Peter Parker — in a Discussion paper some 40 odd years later!) that what in present day business jargon would be referred to as a 'Rolling Programme' should be pursued in the national interest. This was, of course, fine talk in the depressed years of the early 1930s but the report was silent as to how such extension of electrification might be financed.

Also included in the 1931 Weir report were a couple of Charles Merz's proposals and estimates for main line electrification projects. One covered much of the former GN section of the LNER viz: Kings Cross to Doncaster and Leeds, plus Grantham to Nottingham, Boston and Lincoln along with the Doncaster-March route (the 'Joint Line'), Peterborough-Grimsby (the 'East Lincs') and (most surprisingly) the Mablethorpe and Skegness branches, also Coningsby Junction to Bellwater Junction (a relative backwater!). The other proposition covered the LMS West Coast main line between Crewe and Carlisle, and Weaver Junction to Liverpool, including (incredibly) the Windermere Branch and lines to Morecambe/Heysham! They did, however, make the very valid point that a massive programme of electrification might be preferable to one of fragmentation and, oddly enough, a Royal Commission on Transport in a report published in 1930 also supported the philosophy of railway electrification. Needless to say, these two rather extreme forms of electrification 'kite flying' failed even to reach the proverbial drawing board.

The government of the day, under the Railways (Agreement) Act of 1935 did, however, decide to give some financial assistance towards electrification (in the shape of long term loans at favourable rates of interest), and in 1936 the LNER launched two 1500v DC schemes, namely Manchester-Sheffield/Wath (MSW) and Liverpool Street-Shenfield, but fate intervened yet again as the outbreak of World War II in 1939 caused work on both to be suspended. It subsequently fell to British Railways, following nationalisation in 1948, to complete these two projects — the Shenfield being the first to become operational from 25th September 1949 (afterwards extended to Chelmsford and Southend Victoria in 1956). The MSW scheme was implemented in stages between 1952 and 1955, and subsequently extended to the newly opened Tinsley Yard in 1965.

During the mid-1950s the British Transport Commission (BTC) 'Modernisation Plan' was in full swing, and in his report dated December 1954 the Chairman, Sir Brian Robertson, foreshadowed the demise of steam traction in favour of electric and diesel locomotives/multiple units. He proposed, among other things, electrification of the ECML from "Kings Cross to Doncaster and Leeds and (possibly) York."

Sir Brian did not specify DC or AC — just 'electrification' in its broadest sense — because immediately following nationalisation the BTC had been looking very closely at the merits of the two systems. A joint BTC/London Transport advisory committee set up in 1948, recommended in 1951 that 1500v DC continue to be norm for future main line electrification schemes, but by the time the 'Electrification of Railways' report was published in March 1956 the BTC had firmly decided in favour of 25kv AC. They had already asked the Minister of Transport to approve their decision so that the Railways (Standardisation of Electrification) Order 1932 — which had arisen out of the 1931 Weir report and specified DC as the standard — might be amended or revoked.

The BTC's decision to adopt 25kv AC was subsequently recognised in a Government White Paper (HMSO Cmd 813) in July 1959 which outlined a reappraisal of the 1955 Modernisation Plan. It quoted the change of policy as "--- enabling electrification to be carried out more quickly, more simply and at lower cost." The need for conversion of the Liverpool Street-Chelmsford/Southend Victoria system from DC to AC was also touched upon (this work took place in 1960), but more importantly the White Paper stressed that only one of two main line routes proposed for electrification would now be progressed, ie the LM Region's WCML between Euston and Birmingham/Crewe/Manchester and Liverpool. The Kings Cross-Leeds ('and possibly York') ECML scheme was put back (quote) to "sometime after 1964"!

Then following in the wake of the 'Reshaping of British Railways' report of 1963 (the 'Beeching' report), a further BRB document entitled 'Development of Trunk Routes' appeared in 1965. The MSW route was one of two (out of four) Trans-Pennine routes selected for development; the basis of this selection included a prognosis (crystal ball gazing?) on probable 1984 traffic levels. Forecasted MSW trunk trains flow-densities for 1984 could not have been known with any degree of certainty (though it might well have been suspected?) that combined NCB/CEGB/BR strategies then being developed for concentrated bunker loading facilities, with even larger base load power stations using MGR trains almost in a 'conveyor belt' fashion, would remove much of its staple traffic. (Also it could not possibly have been foreseen that radical and enforced financial changes would arise some 15 years later whereby Railfreight would have to stand on its own feet without any government subsidy.)

One of the main causes for selection of the MSW route was that it was 'electrified'. A postscript even thought aloud that scope existed for the MSW to extend westwards to Liverpool via the CLC route — yet just over a decade later the pendulum swung the other way. A Trans-Pennine Route Strategy re-appraisal conducted during the late 1970s revealed that traffic flows had undergone a radical change, not to mention the financial goal posts having been moved. (Since publication of the 1965 Trunk Routes Development report the freight subsidy was eliminated from the end of 1977.) The study concluded there was one east-west route too many, and by then, because the MSW was the only one of its kind, the writing was on the wall. The seemingly unavoidable end came in 1981 when during the early hours of Saturday 18th July the last westbound electrically hauled freight wended its way through Woodhead Tunnel and the MSW was no more.

To be completely objective, and admittedly with the benefit of hindsight, circumstances forced the railway management of the day into an unenviable situation — not entirely one of their own making —

whereby the MSW closure, regrettable as it was, became inevitable. Just like the Shildon-Newport de-electrification some 40 odd years earlier the staple traffic flow which originally formed the justification to electrify had been eroded. Even worse, in the MSW's case the very system of 1500v DC first developed, tried and tested on the Shildon-Newport line, and subsequently supported by three official Committees of Enquiry, had become obsolete as the inexorable march of progress decreed 25kv to be the preferred option.

Even so, we can at long last derive satisfaction secure in the knowledge that ECML electrification *is* going to happen, albeit some 70 years later and in a form altogether different from how it was first envisaged in the early 1920s. After May 1991, when Kings Cross-Edinburgh electric services are due to commence, it will then be possible to see electrically hauled express trains hurtling past the site of the former Simpasture Branch overbridge north of Aycliffe, where once the Shildon-Newport electrics trundled across the top of the ECML. If those early pioneers, Merz and Raven, had still been around today surely they would have approved.

8. ELECTRIC LOCOMOTIVES AND THE ELECTRIFIED SYSTEM

The ten strong fleet of 0-4+4-0 1500 volts DC electric locomotives was numbered 3-12 inclusive; Nos 1 and 2 being the Newcastle Quayside Branch electrics of 1905. They were built at Darlington North Road Works during 1914 (following a Works Order placed on 6th May 1913), and with the exception of No 12 were taken into stock in December 1914. No 3 was officially photographed in 'workshops grey' livery on 11th May 1914 and the fleet duly despatched to Shildon (except No 12) on 18th June 1915. The electric locomotives were stabled in the specially adapted No 3 Roundhouse at Shildon. The exception, No 12, had its bodywork completed along with the rest but it was not finished until December 1919 and entered traffic on 17th May 1920.

Following trial energisation of the first electrified section for testing purposes from 21st June 1915, Nos 3-10 were regarded as being in traffic between 21st/24th June, and No 11 from 22nd December.

Original NER/ LNER No	LNER May 1946 Re-numbering	BR 1948 Number
3	6490	26502
4	6491	26503
5	6492	26504
6	6493	26505
7	6494	26506
8	6495	26507
9	6496	26508
10	6497	26509
11	6498	26510
12	6499	26511

After the cessation of electric working from 1st January 1935 the ten electrics remained at Shildon until closure of that depot from 8th July 1935, when they were transferred to Darlington (Stooperdale) Paint Shops and stored there until

Fig 65   Electric Locomotive No 8 at Shildon.   *(Courtesy: K.L. Taylor collection)*

1947 when they were removed to the Electric Car Sheds at South Gosforth.

Withdrawal from service (except for No 11) occurred on 21st August 1950 when the whole fleet was sold to Messrs Wanty & Co of Catcliffe near Rotherham for scrapping, with the exception of Nos 5 and 11. No 5 was subsequently scrapped by BR at Darlington, the bogies being retained as spares for No 11 which had been rebuilt at Doncaster Works during 1941/42.

The LNER had originally planned to utilise Shildon-Newport locomotives on the MSW electrification, most probably as banking engines. No 11 was selected for rebuilding at Doncaster in 1941 and by the time the conversion was completed in December 1942 its general appearance had been significantly altered. It will be noted from the official photograph taken on 11th October 1944 (fig 66) that one centre pantograph had replaced the original pair, and the position of the cab door was changed from centre to right hand on each side. Electric marker lights and additional sandboxes were also provided.

From 25th August 1949, No 11 (by now BR No 26510) was employed as the depot shunting pilot at Ilford Car Sheds (following the Shenfield electrification), and from 1st January 1959 it was taken into departmental stock and renumbered 100. It was withdrawn from 4th November 1960 (following the Shenfield voltage conversion to AC), stored at Goodmayes until officially condemned on 9th April 1964 and afterwards taken to Doncaster Works to be broken up.

No 3 hauled the inaugural train on the first day of electric operation between Shildon (Middridge Sidings) and Bowesfield West box (where traction was changed to steam) on 1st July 1915.

No 5 was unique in that it retained its NER livery and distinctive numberplate right through to the end (despite having paid a visit to Darlington Works between 16th November 1929 and 18th January 1930 for heavy repairs after running 46000 miles).

No 6 (with dynamometer car) was used on the acceptance trials which took place on 2nd April 1916, and subsequently was involved in a collision with P2 (J26) 0-6-0 No 1208 at Carlton (Redmarshall) on 29th December 1922.

No 8 was fitted with a De-Normanville clear view screen set in half the driver's front window at each end. This consisted of a rapidly rotating glass circle which threw off rainwater. It was used extensively on the bridges of ships, particularly naval craft, and No 8 retained this fitting to the end. No 8 was used

Fig. 66   Electric Locomotive No 11 in LNER days after modification at Doncaster Works 11th October 1944.
(Subsequently renumbered 6498.)
(Courtesy: NRM, York)

Fig. 67   Electric Locomotive No 11 in BR days as 26510 at Ilford, 27th February 1954. (Subsequently renumbered Departmental 100.)   *(Courtesy: E.V. Fry)*

Fig 68   An ignominious end for Electric Locomotive No 5 (BR 26504) at Darlington North Road scrapyard 18th March 1951. (Note still in NER livery complete with original works plate.)
(Courtesy: J.W. Armstrong)

Fig 69   Trial of strength (1) — NER class T3 (Q7) 0-8-0 903 (BR 63462) on test train with dynamometer car waiting to leave Newport for Shildon 5th October 1921.   *(Courtesy: NRM, York)*

Fig 70   Trial of strength (2) — Electric Locomotive No 8 on test train with dynamometer car also waiting to leave Newport a week later on 12th October 1921.   *(Courtesy: NRM, York)*

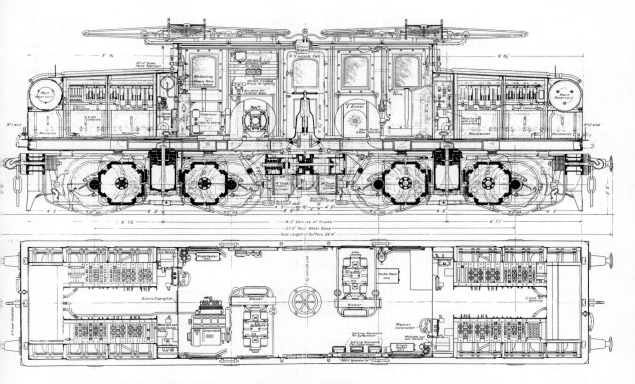

Drawing 12   Side Elevation of Shildon-Newport electric locomotive.   *(Courtesy: Railway Gazette)*

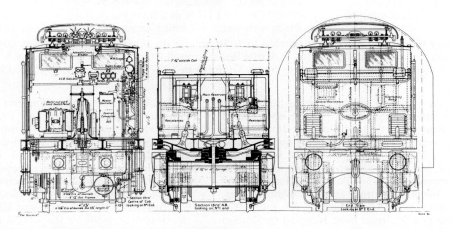

Drawing 13   End view of Shildon-Newport electric locomotive.   *(Courtesy: Railway Gazette)*

in dynamometer car trials during October 1921 when its performance was measured against T3 (Q7) No 903. Resulting from these practical tests the permitted loadings were raised from 1000T to 1400T, with a maximum of 70 wagons, as from 29th November 1922.

No 9 took part in the Railway Centenary procession from Stockton to Darlington of Thursday 2nd July 1925 (as Exhibit No 13) hauled by J71 0-6-0T No 317.

The Shildon-Newport fleet (except No 11) was classified EB1 from 4th October 1945 (ie electric bankers) but by 1949 they had reverted to class EF1 (ie electric freight). Following the LNER's re-appraisal of MSW electrification after World War II, a decision was taken against further conversion of the Shildon-Newport locomotives, thus they were withdrawn in 1950. Sir Nigel Gresley had already developed a mixed traffic and more powerful MSW prototype which appeared in 1941 as No 6701. Its rated power output was 1870 hp (one hour) or 1740 hp (continuous) which made it superior to Raven's 1100 hp design, and pending completion of the MSW scheme, 6701 (by now 6000) was loaned to the Netherlands State Railways (where it affectionately received the name *Tommy*) between 1947 and 1952. *Tommy* became BR No 26000, and was subsequently scrapped at Crewe during 1970.

It is also of interest to record that in July 1928, Gresley proposed the conversion of one Shildon-Newport locomotive to diesel-electric propulsion, but retaining the original bogies. A new super-structure would have housed a 'Beardmore' 1000 hp diesel engine working at 900 rpm and an English Electric generator with 1500v DC output. As the generator was to be located in the centre cab portion, it would have been necessary to construct end driving cabs. In the event Beardmores appear to have had second thoughts and the conversion order placed with English Electric was cancelled in November 1929.

Technical Data — Electric Locomotives Nos 3-12

Type	0-4+4-0 (Bo-Bo)
Voltage	1500v DC
System	Overhead collection
Motors (4)	275 hp each
Output	1100 hp (one hour) 635 hp (continuous)
Drive	Straight — Twin Gear
Gear Ratio	4.5 to 1
Bogie Wheels	4'0" diameter
Wheelbase	27'0" (8'9"+9'6"+8'9")
Length over Buffers	39'4"
Weight	74T 8C
Brakes	Westinghouse
Tractive Capacity	1400T @ 25 mph
Tractive Effort (1 hour)	19600 lbs) subsequently quoted by
Tractive Effort (continuous)	10400 lbs) LNER as 28000 lbs
Livery	Black with single red lining originally, all black from 1917

Notes: After rebuilding, No 11 was uprated to 1256 hp and the maximum tractive effort quoted as having been increased from 28000 lbs to 37600 lbs. Its overall length actually decreased by 3¾" to 39' 0¼". It was moved from Doncaster to South Gosforth in 1947 before going to Ilford in 1949.

Sir Vincent Raven's prototype main line electric express passenger locomotive (No 13) was ordered from Darlington North Road Works on 26th January 1921, the electrical equipment being supplied and installed by Metropolitan-Vickers Ltd. It was out-shopped in May 1922 and apart from various trials and/or demonstration runs on the Shildon-Newport section it never performed any real work. Its best known exploit occurred on Sunday 4th June 1922 when hauling a test train from Newport to Shildon composed of 17 coaches plus dynamometer car, total weight 460T; it maintained an average speed of 42 mph climbing the 1 in 103 gradient approaching Carlton South and averaged 58 mph up the lengthy 1 in 230 rise beyond Carlton through Stillington.

No 13 appeared in 'workshops grey' livery and it is not known whether it was ever painted in NER 'saxony green'. It was, however, painted in LNER green during 1925 prior to taking part in the Railway Centenary procession of 2nd July 1925 (as Exhibit No 32) when it was hauled by J71 0-6-0T No 1163. Apart from being seen at occasional exhibitions during the early 1930s, No 13 languished at Darlington (Stooperdale) Paint Shops (where it was joined by the Shildon-Newport locomotives in July 1935) and subsequently moved to South Gosforth in 1947 (its LNER classification was EE1).

Renumbered 6999 by the LNER in May 1946, No 13 finally became BR No 26600 in 1948. It was withdrawn along with its Shildon-Newport counter-parts on 21st August 1950 and sold to the same scrap merchants (Wantys of Catcliffe). Its final journey to Catcliffe (situated on the former Sheffield District Railway) took place on 15th December 1950.

Technical Data — Electric Locomotive No 13

Type	4-6-4 (2-Co-2)
Voltage	1500v DC
System	Overhead collection
Motors (3 pairs)	300 hp each
Output	1800 hp
Drive	Cup and Quill
Bogie Wheels	3'7¼" diameter
Driving Wheels	6'8" diameter
Wheelbase (rigid)	16'0"
Length over Buffers	53'6"
Weight	102T 0C
Brakes	Westinghouse
Tractive Effort (1 hour)	15900 lbs @ 43 mph 1800 hp) subsequently quoted by
Tractive Effort (continuous)	9480 lbs @ 51.5 mph 1300 hp) LNER as 28000 lbs
Livery	LNER Green (1925)

When the electrification scheme was finally completed in 1916 only certain running lines and sidings between Shildon and Newport were wired for electric traction. For example, between Simpasture and Middridge boxes only the down (westbound) passenger line was electrified. This was because up (eastbound) electrically hauled mineral trains all started from Middridge departure group in Shildon Laden Yard and reached Simpasture Junction independently from the up passenger line. Similarly, only the down (eastbound) passenger line between Bowesfield and Thornaby East was electrified, the reason for this being that if anything went wrong on the electrified mineral lines, Bowesfield could still run a down electric train off the 'Eden' via the passenger line for Thornaby East to turn it into Erimus Yard (provided there was an empty reception available!). Only certain parts of Erimus Yards were wired, though other locations around Newport where loads were detached or empties picked up were made accessible to the electrics, such as Whitwells Sidings, North Receptions, Klondyke and Middle Junction (Foreshore).

To accommodate the additional equipment required for isolation and section breaking purposes, extensions were added to certain signal boxes viz:

> Middridge
> Simpasture
> Stillington Station
> Carlton South
> Bowesfield West
> Bowesfield
> Tees Bridge
> Thornaby East
> Thornaby Ironworks
> Old River

The signal box extensions were all of wooden construction except at Stillington Station and Carlton South (Redmarshall South) where they were brick built. At Stillington Junction and Foreshore boxes sufficient space apparently existed to house the electrical equipment without the need to construct an extension. Other boxes like Shildon and Carlton Station (Redmarshall) never had isolation equipment provided, though such equipment also existed at No 3 Roundhouse, Shildon West shunters cabin and the two sub-stations at Aycliffe and Newport. The section breakers were operated by signal box type levers grouped into a separate frame and they were used as and when directed by Control to isolate certain sections for maintenance purposes, engineering operations or during an emergency.

Outside inspection and maintenance of overhead wires and electrification structures was performed by technical staff working from specially constructed tower wagons, either hauled or propelled by a steam locomotive, usually within weekend possession periods.

Two examples of the signal box electrification extensions still remain at the time of writing, namely at Bowesfield (wood) and Stillington Station (brick).

9. FREIGHT OPERATIONS AND SIGNALLING MISCELLANY

9.1 Mineral Train Working — Control and Operations

Only a relatively small proportion of the North East's local freight and mineral trains actually appeared in the working timetables because much of the originating coal, coke and limestone traffic was conveyed under 'mineral leading' arrangements. In the very early days coal was moved from collieries with scant regard to the prevailing conditions elsewhere which inevitably resulted in congestion, delay, poor wagon utilisation, empty wagon supply difficulties and even chaos as the traffic volume grew commensurate with the pace of mid/late 19th century industrial development. Shipment of coal was also a growth activity in the North-East, right up to the outbreak of World War I; the total output of the Durham coalfield which had reached the 20 million tons mark by 1870, doubled itself 40 years later. Clearly this substantial and rising work load for the NER demanded the introduction of a regulatory system, thus 'mineral leading' was evolved designed to achieve a disciplined yet flexible pattern of operation.

For shipment traffic, the NER 'mineral leading' system was aimed at matching forecasted colliery outputs with prevailing shipping situations at ports and stocks on hand at associated holding sidings awaiting shipment. Hence the main Yard Masters, in close liaison with their counterparts, the 'Staiths Superintendents' at major coal shipment points, would arrange the next day's 'mineral leading' train programme and requisition their local engine sheds to provide power (the daily 'engine order') and crews (the daily 'docket') to move the traffic — and just as important to redistribute empty wagons. This was the first step towards the eventual extension of mineral leading principles to the multiplicity of local freight and trip workings then found throughout the industrial parts of the North East.

By the early-1900s, the sheer intensity of freight working within the Tees-side industrial complex paved the way towards the introduction of a traffic control system. Over 100 furnaces were continuously in blast, some 30 ironstone mines in Cleveland were between them producing around 6 million tons of iron ore per annum, and approximately 5,000 wagons of coal, coke, iron ore and other raw materials (such as limestone) plus a similar number of empty wagons, required movement every weekday

— before one even got around to thinking about outwards goods traffic in finished iron and steel products. The NER, as part of their 1908-1911 reorganisation of freight marshalling activities at Newport and Erimus yards, introduced their first control office located within the Yard Master's accommodation at Newport. The Yard Master's office was situated near to the Old River (between the two main groups of yards) and the building survived until the major Tees Yards reconstruction took place in 1962/3.

Newport Control, which opened on November 14th 1910, closely monitored the movement of all freight trains between Bowesfield and Skinningrove, controlled the local trip workings, and manipulated freight traffic flows around Tees-side. Due regard was paid to the raw materials requirements and the finished production output of major industrial users, but most particularly the empty wagon supply for iron and steel works needed to be effectively organised. Each afternoon the overall traffic situation was assessed, and loading forecasts obtained from collieries, quarries, ironstone mines and so on. Tomorrow's mineral leading programme, and the Cleveland mines turns schedules were duly formulated and motive power/train crew resources requisitioned by means of the daily 'engine order' and 'docket'.

The engine sheds supplying power and crews for Tees-side freight and mineral turns were Newport, Middlesbrough, Stockton and Haverton Hill and the local 'workhorses' were mainly an assortment of Q5/Q6/J27/J26/J25 types — classes T and P in NER days.

Following World War I when times became really bad and traffic levels declined alarmingly from 1920 onwards, the LNER North Eastern Area in its quest to contain working costs, yet improve efficiency and maximise the utilisation of resources, set up a new Middlesbrough District Control organisation which opened on October 6th 1930. The 1930 Middlesbrough Control which supervised a much larger area than the original Newport installation was located in the then Dock Street Offices of the District Goods and Dock Manager Middlesbrough. Also on 30th November 1931 the Darlington District Control office opened, situated in the then District Superintendent's office block in Park Lane alongside Bank Top station, and following yet another organisational upheaval in 1936, which combined the Darlington and Middlesbrough operating districts, the Darlington Control was enlarged and overtook the functions of Middlesbrough Control as from 2nd June 1936.

During 1937 in conjunction with an increasing trend towards block coal train working direct from collieries to steel works which reduced the marshalling activity at Newport, the LNER (North Eastern Area) introduced a bonus incentive scheme for what was known as the 'Tees-side North Collieries' group of trains. Bonus schemes for some local pickup types of trains had been selectively introduced from around 1931 but the North Collieries scheme — which was effective from 22nd March 1937 — certainly proved its worth during World War II when Tees-side's railway system, and the staff who ran it, rose to the occasion and handled massively increased volumes of traffic often in difficult conditions.

Under the North Eastern bonus schemes train crews were encouraged by financial inducements, derived from terminals and point to point running allowances, to get through a set amount of work — as determined by the daily 'docket'. They were also excused the chore of stabling their engines on return to shed and allowed to go home early upon completion of scheduled work. The tempo of local operation was considerably improved under bonus conditions and vast quantities of traffic could be moved efficiently, but following nationalisation in 1948 the then Railway Executive wanted to eliminate the North Eastern Region freight train bonus schemes — perhaps because they were 'different'? The NE Region management of the day were, however, able to successfully demonstrate that to move the same amount of traffic under non-bonus conditions (in the early 1950s) would have required something like an increase of one third in locomotives and crews, and needless to say the matter was not pursued at that point in time! (The traditional bonus schemes were subsequently swallowed up in a national scheme during the 1960s — in rather different conditions following dieselisation — and eliminated altogether in the 1970s resulting from national negotiations with the railway trade unions which consolidated bonus into basic pay, but that is another story!) Anti-bonus opinion said — perhaps with some justification? — that the locomotives were subjected to above average maintenance and repair frequencies and a greater risk of accidents existed due to allegedly 'slip shod' methods of working. Certainly some drivers tended to 'flog' their engines (and their firemen!) but it was never really proved that bonus working around Tees-

side, in itself, produced more derailments and collisions than would otherwise have been the case.

During the early 1950s the daily average number of bonus *mineral* turns operating in and around Shildon-Newport territory was:

Middlesbrough	30
Newport	11
Stockton	8
Haverton Hill	13
West Auckland	2
Darlington	4
	68

By 1960 following the establishment of a completely new steam depot at Thornaby in 1958 there were still some 36 daily mineral turns on average, supplemented by approximately 20 West Auckland turns. The increase in West Auckland turns was mainly due to surplus power and crews becoming available by the removal of freight traffic over the Stainmore route to Tebay in 1960 — prior to complete closure of the line in 1962. The West Auckland men, along with their colleagues at West Hartlepool, were to go on and perform sterling work with their ageing (and ailing!) fleet of locomotives right up to the end of steam. West Auckland shed finally closed from 2nd February 1964 and a train crew depot (using Thornaby based diesel locomotives) was set up at Shildon yard until it too was swallowed up by Thornaby and Darlington depots as the traffic in South West Durham fell away in the late 1960s.

Diesel locomotives came to Thornaby and Darlington depots during the early/mid-1960s and steam was gradually phased out until it finally disappeared from the Tees-side scene following withdrawal of the last Q6 from West Hartlepool on 17th September 1967. Thornaby shed first absorbed the work of Middlesbrough and Newport sheds from 1st June 1958 (officially opened 5th June 1958), and from 13th June 1959 the two remaining Tees-side sheds, Stockton and Haverton Hill, were also closed.

To update the story, the NE Region's management reorganisation of 1960 resulted in the creation of a Traffic Manager's position based at Middlesbrough (later called Divisional Manager) which involved construction of a new office block situated above part of the station forecourt, and formally opened as 'Zetland House' on 22nd July 1960. The revised organisation enabled a centralisation of operating and commercial managerial/administration functions to be achieved; also a new Middlesbrough Control office replaced the older Darlington Control. Nevertheless, it was not to be very long before the Middlesbrough Divisional organisation disappeared in the wake of the Beeching

Fig 71   Class 37 6700 (37119) hauling a mid-1960s freight from Hartlepool to Tees Yard at Thornaby Station.
(Courtesy: Author's collection)

era; as from 5th December 1966, its functions were absorbed by an enlarged Newcastle Division as a prelude to the Eastern and North Eastern Regional merger which took place on 1st January 1967.

For a while Middlesbrough Control continued to function, latterly in a very much modified form, until the advent of TOPS in 1975. TOPS (Total Operations Processing System) heralded a whole new concept of freight traffic and rolling stock control by means of computerised techniques, and the system now forms an integral part of railway operations and engineering management having subsequently been extended into the fields of locomotive and wagon maintenance. Then in 1984 the Divisional organisations themselves disappeared, and under a two-tier management structure British Rail's Area Manager Middlesbrough (located Zetland House) presided over a domain which was still largely recognisable as the territory covered by the erstwhile Middlesbrough Division.

However, around the time of writing it emerged that even further organisational changes were afoot, which resulted in a revised Area Management structure at Middlesbrough covering 'Tees-Tyne' freight activities (ie both Tees-side and Tyneside freight but excluding Durham/Northumberland Coal which had its own separate management at Sunderland), with the local passenger business now being managed from Newcastle. The whole economic and industrial scenario is completely different from that of bygone days as the sheer volume and density of freight and mineral traffic no longer exists. 'Quantity' has tended to be replaced by 'quality' thus a multiplicity of collieries, iron and steelworks, quarries, private sidings and even marshalling yards has disappeared. In turn, a radically changed management structure has, of necessity, evolved in order to ensure that the 1990s kind of freight network in this part of the North East is run in a cost-effective yet business orientated manner appropriate to present day customer requirements.

For instance, whilst the once seemingly endless procession of freight and mineral trains that one could see around places like Bowesfield, Stockton, Redmarshall, Stillington and so on — particularly during World War II — has gone for ever, it is pleasing to record that a new generation of coal trains ply between the Durham Coast collieries and York (via Stockton) conveying loads in excess of 1,000 tons apiece bound for the big power stations in the Aire Valley. Hauled mostly by class 56 diesel locomotives and formed by modern MGR wagons (Shildon-built of course) these trains represent the ultimate in bulk coal movement by rail. Even more recently MGR coal trains now run between Northumberland/Durham collieries and ICI Wilton.

9.2 Signalling Arrangements

In the very early days of railways when the horse reigned supreme, it was very much a case of every man for himself and signalling as such was virtually non-existent, but as the original single track routes were doubled and locomotive haulage superseded the horse, movements tended to be regulated under a time interval system. Then along came the electric telegraph and soon this new means of communication was adapted for railway signalling purposes.

By 1854 the S&D had installed a primitive kind of telegraph system (sometimes referred to as 'Bains Block') to regulate the passage of trains through Shildon Tunnel. The 1854 and 1862 issues of the S&D Rule Book both contained special instructions for the safe working of trains through the tunnel; for example, Rule 134 of the 1862 book said: "Immediately a train enters at either end, the signal to stop must be put on, to stop approaching traffic, and so remain until 'all's right' is announced by the telegraph. In the event of the telegraph being out of order, a pilot engine and Staff must be used to precede each train."

In 1865 the NER appointed a Signalling Superintendent called Alfred O. Walker who had a system patented which soon became known as 'Walkers Block'. This was an early form of what later became 'Block Telegraph' (or 'Absolute Block' as we know it today) and it was introduced between Darlington and Shildon on 31st October 1865, using "Walkers Patent electro-magnetic telegraph semaphore instruments". Fortunately an example of this instrument has survived which can be seen at the Darlington North Road Railway Museum.

The introduction of block working gathered momentum throughout NER territory during the 1870s following the Directors having made a conscious decision by May 1871 to introduce the 'Block Telegraph System' and commence 'block classes' for the tuition of potential signalmen — who for some years afterwards were required in large numbers. The North Eastern thus became involved in the wholesale provision of new 'signal cabins' together with huge quantities of associated signalling equipment, not only to cope with the introduction of block working, interlocking and so on, but also to cater for expansion of the infrastructure to meet the ever increasing demand for additional rail facilities in the contemporary situation of industrial growth — particularly in the Tees-side and County Durham area.

By 1880 absolute block had become fairly universal on NER passenger lines and in this respect it is worthy of note that the legislation which actually made block systems on passenger carrying lines compulsory by law was not enacted until 1889. This act (known as the Regulation of Railways Act 1889) also required railway companies to install properly interlocked lever frames in signal cabins, though here again the NER were well advanced having fitted facing point locks and mechanically operated wedges from 1869 onwards. (A previous Railway Regulation Act of 1873 required companies to make periodic returns regarding progress in this respect.) On NER lines used exclusively for goods traffic most of the lines not worked to any block system were gradually converted to a form of permissive working, using Tyers Recording Instruments (known throughout the North East as 'Recording Block') which allowed successive trains to follow each other into an occupied section under caution acceptance conditions.

Nevertheless, it is of interest to recall certain comments made by a couple of Board of Trade Inspecting Officers following investigation into certain accidents. For example, following a collision near Thornaby Road level crossing on 12th November 1872 when a down goods train ran into the back of a passenger train which was standing at a signal awaiting admittance to South Stockton station's single platform (which was occupied by an up train), Capt H.W. Tyler in his report dated 22nd November 1872 remarked "--- this section of the NER is crowded with traffic. Preparations are being made for introduction of the block telegraph system of working and the sooner they are completed, together with the extra accommodation such as additional lines and sidings, and the extra appliances that are necessary for carrying out that system, the better ---". Capt Tyler went on to say (about South Stockton) "--- a general scheme for improvement at the station should be carried out ---." Then Lieut Col C.S. Hutchinson right at the end of his report dated 5th February 1874 into an accident which occurred at Bowesfield on 21st December 1873 when a down passenger train ran into the rear portion of a stationary freight train which was detaching into South Stockton goods yard, made the pointed comment "--- the interlocking and signal arrangements at Bowesfield Junction are of an antiquated and incomplete character ---".

Soon after these two accidents the NER embarked upon a major track widening scheme between Stockton Cut (half a mile west of Bowesfield in the Eaglescliffe direction) and Newport East, which also included the construction of Newport Yard, followed by a new island platform station at South

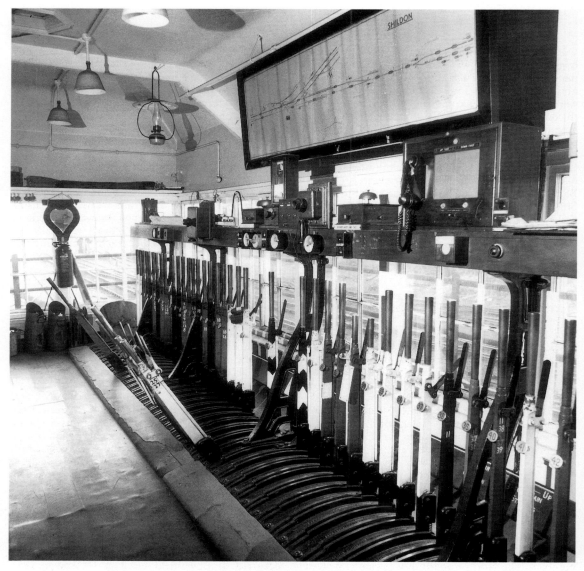

Fig. 72   Shildon signal box interior 11th July 1979 showing part of McKenzie & Holland Pattern 16 frame of 55 levers installed during 1928. (Originally called Shildon Junction, this box dates from 1884. It was renamed Shildon South in 1928 and became 'Shildon' in 1967.)   *(Courtesy: British Rail)*

Stockton (later Thornaby) and an additional viaduct over the Tees for the mineral lines. So it is fair to say that the exhortations of Messrs Tyler and Hutchinson were duly heeded! In fact, signalling alterations and various other improvements — particularly between Bowesfield and Newport — proceeded almost continuously from 1876 to around 1910. Actually from the turn of the century up to the 1915 electrification much of the original signalling equipment on the lines covered by this book was gradually modernised; old boxes were either extended or replaced by completely new structures, and lever frame renewals frequently took place. However, with the passage of time it is becoming increasingly difficult to trace with certainty the precise history of every signal box, though a fairly detailed summary of what is known to the author has been produced, for the record, as an appendix to this chapter.

The three remaining boxes are at Shildon (1887), Stillington Station (1884) and Bowesfield (1905); the Thornaby and Tees Yard area being controlled by Tees Box (1962/3) which is situated in the Down Yard tower opposite the site of the former (1908) Old River box. Both Shildon and Stillington boxes are the second ones to be built there but Bowesfield is the third. The first 'Bowesfield Lane' box apparently dated from around 1863 and was located on the down (north) side of the line between the junctions with the Hartburn curve and Stockton Wharf branch. (This was the installation described as "antiquated and of incomplete character" by Lieut Col Hutchinson in 1874.) The second 'Bowesfield Junction' box was situated on the up (south) side of the tracks slightly to the east of the present box and it dated from 1876 (Board of Trade inspection date October 9th 1876). At that time there was a level crossing here over ten sets of rails! — but this was replaced by a subway the same year following the diversion of Bowesfield Lane, which passes underneath the railway by means of a bridge still bearing the inscription 'MDCCCLXXVI'.

Finally, the 1876 box was replaced by the present structure situated slightly to the west and also on the up (south) side of the line. The new box, brought into use during March 1905, was inspected by Col Yorke on 8th June 1905, though since then there have been so many alterations that the present day track layout and signalling equipment bears little resemblance to the original!

All traces of the various other Shildon-Newport and Wellfield Branch signal boxes have long since vanished. One can now only visit some of the abandoned sites, and perhaps pause for a while to reflect upon the considerable degree of change which has taken place — particularly over the last twenty-five years.

Fig 73   Class V3 2-6-2T 67688 passing Thorpe Thewles with diverted Middlesbrough-Newcastle train Sunday 22nd October 1950. Note 1906 wooden signal cabin on up platform and bottom of original 1878 brick built cabin in right background.
(Courtesy: J.W. Armstrong)

APPENDIX

Details of Signal Boxes and Gate Boxes summarised in line order, together with brief historical notes

A Summary

1 Shildon to Newport

(Shildon Works)

Masons Arms GB

Shildon (South) SB (junction from Bishop Auckland direction)

Middridge SB

Simpasture Jct SB (junction to Heighington/Darlington direction)

(present day Newton Aycliffe Halt)

Simpasture East SB)
School Aycliffe GB) (site of wartime stations
Demons Bridge SB) for ROF Aycliffe)

(A167-old A1 road bridge)

Travellers Rest SB/GB (Durham County Council roadways depot)

Ricknall Mill GB

(site of bridge over ECML)

(site of Aycliffe sub-station)

(A1(M) trunk road)

Preston Lane GB/SB

Elstob Lane GB/SB

Bishopton Lane GB

Stillington North SB (junction from Sedgefield/Ferryhill direction)

Stillington Station SB

Redmarshall (Carlton) Station SB

(site of Carlton West Jct) (junction to Redmarshall East/Norton West)

Redmarshall South SB (junction from Redmarshall North/Wellfield)

(site of Bowesfield West SB) (junction to Hartburn West Line 1901/3)

(site of bridge over Leeds Northern Line between Eaglescliffe and Stockton)

Bowesfield SB (junctions from Stockton Cut (Eaglescliffe) and Hartburn)

Tees Bridge SB

Thornaby East SB

Via Erimus/Newport (Tees) Yards	*Via Passenger Lines*
Thornaby Ironworks SB	
Old River SB	Newport West SB
(Tees Yard Power Box)	
Foreshore SB	
Newport East SB	Newport East SB

2 Wellfield to Redmarshall

Wellfield (Castle Eden North Jct) (junction to Hartlepool direction)

(vanished site of bridge over Ferryhill-Hartlepool abandoned line)

Wingate South SB (junction from Wingate Station/Ferryhill direction)

Hurworth Burn SB

Wynyard SB)
Thorpe Thewles SB) (site of Castle Eden Walkway)

(site of Thorpe Thewles Viaduct)

Redmarshall North SB (junction to Redmarshall East/Norton West direction)

(site of bridge over Clarence Railway) (Norton West-Ferryhill)

Redmarshall South SB (junction from Shildon/Ferryhill directions)

B Historical Notes

1 Shildon to Newport

Masons Arms: Level crossing. Not a block post. Wooden hut situated at south west corner of crossing replaced by brick structure 1957 and demolished 1986 following abandonment of Shildon Works Branch (original S&D main line).

Shildon: Present box built 1887. First frame had 40 levers. Was known as Shildon Junction and became Shildon South 18th October 1936 when new Shildon North box opened. Reverted to Shildon box 17th September 1967 after closure of Shildon North. New frame of 55 levers 1928; reduced to 42 in connection with Bishop Auckland (East) box closure on 31st March 1984.

Middridge: Box dated from mid-1870s (previous box near site was called Thickley Sidings). Structure extended 1913 and new frame of 45 levers installed. Box closed along with Shildon Yard 7th January 1935. Remained operative but 'switched out' and unmanned until 30th October 1939 when signalling taken out of use (box subsequently burned down).

Simpasture Junction: Box also dated from mid-1870s. Structure extended 1910 and new frame of 45 levers installed. Branch to Stillington (original Clarence Railway) closed 22nd June 1963. Box closed 21st May 1969.

Simpasture East: LNER wartime box for Simpasture station. Box opened 15th January 1942. (Frame of

34 levers.) Absolute Block working introduced Simpasture-Simpasture East-Demons Bridge same date. Box disused following cessation of munitions factory passenger trains at end of World War II and demolished early 1950s.

School Aycliffe Crossing: Not a block post. Gate box moved from up side of line to down side 1942. Level crossing superseded by new road bridge St Cuthbert's Way 1956 but approach roads not stopped up until 1959.

Demons Bridge: LNER wartime box (frame of 40 levers). Box opened 12th December 1941. Absolute Block working introduced Demons Bridge-Preston Lane-Elstob-Stillington North same date. Box disused following cessation of munitions factory passenger trains at end of World War II. Redundant junction connections removed 1950 and box demolished soon afterwards.

Travellers Rest: Level crossing over old A1 Great North Road. New box built 1909. Since 1935 the signal box was switched out as a block post and worked as a gate box. After Demons Bridge box brought into use on 12th December 1941, it officially became a gate box released by Demons Bridge. Level crossing and gate box closed during 1942 following completion of new A1 road bridge. Box remained in derelict condition well into 1950s. Site now occupied by Durham County Council road maintenance depot.

Ricknall Mill Crossing: Not a block post. Closed 22nd June 1963 following cessation of rail traffic over the Simpasture Branch.

Preston Lane: Originally not a block post, but functioned as such between 12th December 1941 and 20th May 1951 — thereafter reverted to gate box. Closed 22nd June 1963.

Elstob Lane: Originally a gate box, became a block post *c*1899 upon the introduction of 'Recording Block' over the Simpasture Branch, but reverted to gate box *c*1919. Became a block post again 12th December 1941 following introduction of Absolute Block for wartime passenger trains and reverted to gate box 1st March 1947. Closed 22nd June 1963.

Bishopton Lane Crossing: Not a block post. Closed 22nd June 1963.

Stillington Junction: New box with frame of 55 levers 1914. Renamed Stillington North 25th March 1928 following resignalling and introduction of automatic semaphore signals in the Sedgefield-Stillington North section. New frame of 50 levers installed 1959. Simpasture Branch connections put out of use 15th August 1965. Mineral lines to and from Redmarshall officially dispensed with 1st August 1965. Automatic signals removed 1st February 1968. Box closed 18th February 1968 and scheduled for demolition April 1968.

Stillington Station: Present box built 1884. Level crossing stopped up 1932. Box was open for three shifts until 1932 when reduced to 'as required' attendance for pick up goods etc. Officially ceased to be a block post on the mineral lines 23rd May 1962. Mineral lines severed 18th October 1964 in connection with new road bridge underneath the formation east of the box, and officially abandoned 1st August 1965 in connection with resignalling and track realignment. Frame of 32 levers reduced to 7.

Redmarshall Station: Carlton Station box pre-1st July 1923. Box built *c*1885 for track widening scheme and new island platform station which also involved construction of a road bridge to replace former level crossing. Initially the box was a block post on the passenger lines only and the mineral lines block section was Carlton West-Stillington Station. By 1895 the box was extended at the west end and a new frame of 38 levers installed, following the closure of Carlton West box and removal of the junction to Carlton Station. New frame containing 50 levers installed 1955. Layout simplified 1966 following removal of mineral lines and demolition of island platform station together with track realignment. Box closed 25th November 1967 and demolition scheduled to commence 1st April 1968.

Carlton West Junction: Box dated from 1st May 1877 and it controlled a new junction between ex-Clarence Railway 'main line' and spur (officially called the 'Carlton Loop') which joined the Castle Eden Branch at Carlton South. Signalling altered 1885 when another set of connections was installed for the track widening scheme, but box closed 1895 and junctions moved half a mile further west to come under control of Carlton Station box.

Redmarshall South: Carlton South box pre-1st July 1923. This box dated from 1877 when the Castle Eden Branch was under construction. The frame of 15 levers installed 1878 had two added *c*1914, and was replaced by a new one with 20 levers in 1961. Box closed 24th June 1968.

Bowesfield West: New box brought into use 1900 ready for the Hartburn West curve which was only operational between 1901 and 1903. The box remained, latterly to serve a brickyard siding along the abandoned curve site, until closed as a block post 24th October 1932. The frame of 24 levers was reduced to a 3 lever ground frame (situated within the box) and dispensed with *c*1948. Box demolished *c*1952.

Bowesfield: Formerly 'Bowesfield Lane' pre-1876, the first box dated from *c*1863 and was situated on the down side of the tracks between the junctions for Hartburn Curve and Stockton Wharf Branch. The second box dating from 1876 was located on the up side of the line, and the third box (the present one) followed in March 1905 built slightly to the west of the 1876 structure. The frame of 130 levers was modernised and relocked in February 1959, reduced to 45 levers in 1984 and further reduced to 36 in 1986. The box also remotely controls the junctions at Eaglescliffe and Hartburn, and from December 7th 1986 took over what little is now left of the former extensive layouts around Stockton following the closure of North Shore box.

Tees Bridge: The first box dating from 1876 was called 'Stockton Bridge'. It stood on the up side immediately west of the Tees viaduct and controlled the junction for the then new mineral lines from Bowesfield. Renamed Tees Bridge early 1880s. The second box, which contained a frame of 33 levers, dated from 1898 and was situated between the passenger and mineral lines, immediately east of the viaducts. Box closed during the weekend of 25/26th February 1940.

Thornaby West: Stockton West pre-1892. This box originally controlled Thornaby Road level crossing which was replaced by a bridge in 1882. It was resignalled *c*1883 in connection with the new station and track widening scheme, and dispensed with when the new Tees Bridge box opened in 1898. (There was also another level crossing a short distance east of Thornaby Road called Mandale Road. It too disappeared in the 1882 improvements and so far as can be ascertained it was not a block post as such.)

Thornaby East: Stockton East pre-1892. Originally situated on the down side east of the old single platform station, a new box was built on the up side in connection with the 1882 new station. A completely new box which contained a frame of 96 levers, situated at the east end of the island platform between the up and down passenger lines, was opened on 30th August 1908 in association with the Erimus Yard scheme. The lever frame was modernised and relocked in January 1958 (in connection with layout alterations for the new engine shed and diverted passenger lines) and the box was closed on 12th May 1963, under Tees Box alterations Stage 2.

Thornaby Ironworks: Whitwells Junction until *c*1880. The original box controlled the siding connections for Whitwells ironworks (established in 1860) but in association with the passenger line diversions for the Erimus Yard scheme a new box of wooden construction was opened on 30th August 1908. The new box, which contained a frame of 53 levers, controlled down direction traffic only as the up lines were situated some considerable distance away from it on the opposite side of Erimus Yard. Reduced to one shift working in 1932, it was switched out after Whitwells works closed *c*1934 and finally abolished during the summer of 1939.

Newport West: The first Newport West box dating from 1873 was situated east of the Old River bridge; it initially controlled the junction between the passenger lines and the mineral lines, and also the connections leading to the Erimus ironworks which closed *c*1881. (No evidence has yet been found, though it is possible a second enlarged Newport West box was provided when Newport Yard opened in 1875? Certainly a box of this name was closed in 1908 concurrently with the opening of Old River box.) A small wooden box also called Newport West was brought into use on 30th August 1908 though it was merely an intermediate block post (containing a frame of 10 levers) on the diverted passenger lines between Thornaby East and Newport East. Although open for one shift in 1922, it was switched out shortly afterwards and thereafter only manned as required, usually on Bank Holiday Mondays to break the section when a lot of excursions and additional passenger trains ran. This box was dispensed with on 12th January 1958 in association with the Thornaby East alterations and further diversion of the passenger lines to their present alignment.

Old River: This was a new box opened on 30th August 1908 and it replaced the former Newport West. Originally having a frame of 84 levers, the box was enlarged in 1957 and the number of levers increased to 110 in connection with the Thornaby new motive power depot scheme. A precise date for closure has not been established but the box became disused during 1962 after the down side at Newport had been taken over for construction of the new Tees Yard.

Tees Box: This modern power signalling installation is housed within the Tees Down Yard control tower building and it controls the lines from the new (1983) connections west of Thornaby station to the junctions at Newport East. It was brought into use in two stages; stage 1 which involved the closure of Newport East on 12th August 1962, and stage 2 when Thornaby East closed on 12th May 1963.

Foreshore: The first Foreshore box was built in connection with the Newport East Yard scheme of 1875 and it was replaced by a new wooden structure (containing a frame of 75 levers) which came into use during December 1910. A definite closure date has not been traced but the box disappeared in 1962 during the construction of Tees Yard.

Newport East: The original Newport East dated from the 1873 widening scheme and a new box was brought into use in 1903. It had two separate lever frames, one at each side of the box numbered 1-49 and 50-68, and a gate wheel — the level crossing formed the access for Samuelson's works which closed in 1930. Newport East was closed under Tees

Box Stage 1 on 12th August 1962.

2 Wellfield to Redmarshall

Wellfield: Castle Eden North Junction pre-1882. The original box built 1877 was sited on top of the embankment on the up side of the line south of the Durham-Hartlepool road bridge (almost opposite to the junction points). Renamed Wellfield 1882 (when the station was opened). New box opened 1910 fitted with frame of 45 levers, situated at the north end of the up platform. New frame of 20 levers installed 22nd June 1964. Box closed 31st December 1979.

Wingate South: Box and frame of 14 levers dated from 1878. It controlled the junction to and from the curve towards Wingate Station (on the Ferryhill-Hartlepool line). On 6th July 1966 the box was closed and the line severed a short distance southwards. Buffer stops were erected, thus effectively closing the branch for through traffic, though the Wellfield-Wingate South section together with the curve towards Wingate Station remained in use until 30th April 1969 to permit access for Trimdon Grange Colliery.

Hurworth Burn: The original 1878 box was built immediately north of the down platform, but in 1906 it was replaced by a small wooden hut containing a 12 levers frame situated on the up platform. Box closed 17th August 1952.

Wynyard: The original 1878 box was located immediately south of the up platform and in 1914 received a new frame of 20 levers. It was closed on 20th September 1953 and on the same date the Absolute Block system on the branch was replaced by Permissive Block with recording instruments, the sections being Wellfield-Wingate South-Redmarshall North-Redmarshall South. (Absolute Block was retained between Redmarshall North and Redmarshall East boxes.)

Thorpe Thewles: The original 1878 box was located south of the down platform but in 1906 it was replaced by a small wooden hut containing 10 levers situated on the up platform (the base of the old box survived into the 1950s). Box closed 17th August 1952.

Redmarshall North: Carlton North pre-1st July 1923. The original box received a new frame of 14 levers in 1909, and in 1964 yet another new frame of 15 levers was fitted. The box was closed to traffic from 22nd January 1967 and abolished 27th February 1967.

Redmarshall East: Carlton East pre-1st July 1923. The 1878 box received a new frame containing 22 levers in 1903, and the frame was again renewed in 1960 (20 levers). Box closed 22nd January 1967.

Redmarshall South: Carlton South pre-1st July 1923. Original 1877 box closed 24th June 1968.

Notes:

The LNER had a proposal to single the line between Thorpe Thewles and Hurworth Burn with a crossing loop at Wynyard, the method of working to be by Electric Key Token instruments — per a memo to the Board of Directors dated 29th October 1927. In the event, the scheme was not progressed because additional mineral traffic might have arisen from new industrial developments at Billingham SA&N Works (later to become ICI), and a loss of flexibility in working could have resulted. Also, the impending passenger service withdrawal from this line (which took place from 2nd November 1931) meant that porter-signalmen could replace full time signalmen, thus the three intermediate boxes on the branch were switched out of circuit and only opened up when actually required for shunting with the daily pick-up goods or if specially requested by Control. This situation lasted until freight facilities were withdrawn from the three stations (from 2nd April 1951), Thorpe Thewles and Hurworth Burn boxes being abolished on 17th August 1952 followed by Wynyard on 20th September 1953. Between 20th September 1953 and 6th July 1966 (when the line was closed as a through route), the method of working was by Permissive Block between Redmarshall North and Wingate South (extended to apply between Redmarshall South-Wellfield when either or both intermediate boxes were switched out of circuit).

BIBLIOGRAPHY

Jubilee Memorial of the Railway System, J.S. Jeans, 1875

History of the First Public Railway, M. Heavisides, 1912

Trade & Commerce of the North Eastern Railway, NER booklet, 1912

The NER: Its Rise and Development, W.W. Tomlinson, 1914

The Elements of Railway Operating, H.M. Hallsworth, 1914

Railway Electrification — paper read before the NE Coast Institution of Engineers & Shipbuilders on 16th December 1921, Sir V.L. Raven, 1922

Timothy Hackworth and the Locomotive, R. Young, 1923

Control on the Railways, P. Burtt, 1926

North Eastern Electrics, K. Hoole, 1960

Tees New Marshalling Yards, BR NE Region, 1963

A Regional History of Railways in Great Britain: Vol 4 — The North East, K. Hoole, 1965/86

The Electric Railway That Never Was, A.S. Hennessy, 1970

NER Locomotive Sheds, K. Hoole, 1972

Forgotten Railways: North East England, K. Hoole, 1973/84

Tees-side's Economic Heritage, G.A. North, 1975

Railway History in Pictures; The S&D Railway, K. Hoole, 1975

Exploring the S&D Railway, P.W.B. Semmens, 1975

The Byers Green Branch (Clarence Railway), R.S. Abley, 1975

S&D Railway 1825-1975, P.J. Holmes, 1975

The NER 1870-1914: An Economic History, R.J. Irving, 1976

Shildon — Cradle of the Railways, R. Corkin, 1977

North Eastern Branch Lines Since 1925, K. Hoole, 1978

Railway Stations of the North East, K. Hoole, 1985

Cavalcade Reflections, Cavalcade Retrospect, Cavalcade Remembered, BR Eastern Region booklets 1975-1976

Board of Trade/Ministry of Transport Accident Reports, National Railway Museum, York

Board of Trade Inspection Reports and correspondence, Railway Companies Archives, Public Record Office, Kew

Durham County Archives relating to Clarence and North Eastern Railways, Durham County Record Office

North Eastern Railway Magazine, Railway Gazette, The Engineer, Railway Magazine, NRM, York

Northern Echo Railway Centenary special supplement 1925 (reprint 1975), Northern Echo, Darlington